into THE fields

YEAR 1
Sessions 1-10

CATECHIST AND TEACHER FORMATION FOR THE WHOLE COMMUNITY

Basic Catechetical Skills and Attitudes

SPIRITUAL EXERCISES
by **Dan Schutte**

Diana Dudoit Raiche
General Editor

GROWING FAITH
by **Bill Huebsch**

Sr. Maureen Shaughnessy, SC
General Editor

TOOLS FOR TEACHING
by **Alison Berger**

Sr. Edith Prendergast, RSC
General Editor

TWENTY THIRD 23rd PUBLICATIONS

LOYOLA UNIVERSITY NEW ORLEANS

Into the Fields was produced in partnership with Loyola Pastoral Life Center at the Loyola Institute for Ministry

Twenty-Third Publications

A Division of Bayard

One Montauk Avenue, Suite 200

(860) 437-3012 or (800) 321-0411

www.twentythirdpublications.com

ISBN: 1-58595-590-6

ISBN: 978-158595-590-9

Library of Congress Catalog Card Number: 2006903014

Printed in the U.S.A.

Contents

General Introduction

Into the Fields: Catechist and Teacher Formation for the Whole Community is rooted in Scripture, liturgy, and the *Catechism of the Catholic Church* and is based on both the *General Directory for Catechesis* and the *National Directory for Catechesis*. Each volume of this three-year program blends spiritual formation with theological content, theory, practice, and suggestions for age-appropriate activities. Each volume provides you with a comprehensive means of learning and acquiring skills for your teaching ministry. The three volumes are: Year 1, *Basic Catechetical Skills and Attitudes*; Year 2, *Styles of Teaching and Learning*; and Year 3, *Teaching Specific Catholic Topics*.

Each of the ten sessions in each volume begins with a spiritual exercise. These profound experiences combine prayer, meditation, reflection, and a related song inspired by Scripture. A CD with the music for all ten songs accompanies each book.

Next comes *Theological Content*, an essential ingredient for catechist and teacher formation. The ten sessions in each book introduce the topic and recommend the appropriate booklet(s) from the *Growing Faith Project*, a comprehensive and systematic presentation of the faith based on the *Catechism*.

Tools for Teaching is the formal teaching section, providing the connecting link between spiritual growth, content of the faith, and instructional strategies needed to do excellent catechesis.

Following is an outline of the *Into the Fields* "pathway," which shows where each of the above three components fits into the process, plus information about the Large Group Sessions, Ongoing Formation Resources, and available Continuing Education Units.

Step 1. Spiritual Exercises

The *Spiritual Exercises* in *Into the Fields* draw upon the wisdom of St. Ignatius of Loyola. The text was written and the songs composed by Dan Schutte, with Diana Dudoit Raiche as the general editor. The exercises are intended to help you grow in your faith and deepen your relationship with God.

Each exercise is accompanied by a piece of music meant to draw you into the heart of the prayer. The reflections engage your mind and will, stretch your understanding, and draw you closer to the heart of the Lord. A series of "suggestions for use" help you derive the maximum benefit. Each exercise ends with a "colloquy," a prayer conversation with God. The goal here is to be with the God who loves you far more than you know.

Spend about sixty minutes with the exercise, then ten minutes writing notes about your experience. Later, within the large group teaching session, you will be invited to share your personal experiences with others.

Step 2. Theological Content

The *Theological Content* follows the flow of the *Catechism of the Catholic Church* and is complete and comprehensive but in plain English. The author is Bill Huebsch, with Sr. Maureen Shaughnessy, SC, as general editor. Here you will be introduced to the themes covered, and share excerpts from the text.

The purpose here is to study the substance of the Catholic faith in measured, manageable amounts using the *Growing Faith* booklet(s) that apply to the particular session you are covering. Spend at least thirty minutes reading the booklet and doing the exercises and reflections suggested there, taking notes as you proceed. Again, while this may be done privately, you may wish to join with others in this process outside the formal teaching session. Later, within the large group teaching session, you will be invited to share insights and questions.

You will benefit most from your study of the *Growing Faith* booklets if you also reflect on the artwork and call outs (words in large script). Ask yourself: what do these words (or this illustration) mean to me?

Step 3. Tools for Teaching

Tools for Teaching offers you practical catechetical skills and concrete strategies that work in real teaching sessions. The author is Alison Berger, with Sr. Edith Prendergast as the general editor.

The section begins with the goal and objectives and a skill to acquire for the session. The text then sets the tone with an optional introductory story or exercise. Part two helps you reflect on the significance of the topic for catechesis. The three sections of material that follow guide you in implementing the objectives, using theory, practical commentary, and examples, plus strategies for different age levels. Also included are questions for personal use and group discussion to help you integrate what you have learned.

Instructions are provided throughout on how to make the most of the various elements, whether you are studying alone or with a group. Read the appropriate section in *Tools for Teaching* and reflect on the questions before each large group session. This should take about thirty minutes and does not involve any note-taking at this point. The note-taking and sharing will be part of the large group sessions.

Step 4. Large Group Sessions

You will be invited to attend one three-hour-long large group session per topic of *Into the Fields*. This session will follow a specific format through which you will experience and share all three components: *Spiritual Exercises*, *Theological Content*, and *Tools for Teaching*. In this meeting, you will review and share as a group some of the insights and reflections you will be recording in your books. In particular, you will discuss and share the questions in Tools for Teaching. These gatherings will help you see *Into the Fields* as a total program that will help you grow both spiritually and professionally. Also at this meeting, your facilitator will initial or sign your book to indicate that you have satisfactorily completed each session.

Step 5. Ongoing Formation

We highly recommend that you use *RTJ: The Magazine for Catechist Formation* as part of your ongoing formation as a teacher or catechist. Each issue will carry special *Into the Fields* articles as well as many other invaluable features and columns, all geared to enhancing your teaching ministry. We also recommend that you regularly visit the official *Into the Fields* website as part of your ongoing formation (www.intothefields.org). There you will find suggestions for resources, specific activities for your faith formation sessions, and valuable links to other related sites.

Step 6. Continuing Education Units

At the beginning of each trimester (ten sessions) of *Into the Fields*, if you are interested in obtaining two CEUs from Loyola University in New Orleans, you can register through your group facilitator. You will obtain the CEUs once the facilitator determines that you have satisfactorily completed all ten sessions. For more information, visit the website: www.lim.loyno.edu/lplc.

Welcome to Year One

Basic Catechetical Skills and Attitudes

So, you are starting a new year of catechesis! Many experiences await you to help both you and your learners grow as disciples of Christ. Whether you are a brand new catechist or teacher or have already taught for a few years, we hope you will learn from and enjoy the material for this first year of *Into the Fields*.

Basic Catechetical Skills and Attitudes focuses on your spiritual formation and the fundamental skills and knowledge you need to build a solid foundation. Topics covered in this volume include the story of God in your life, the virtue of generosity, planning the learning session, using Scripture effectively, and much more.

Keep this volume close by while you are teaching, as well as while you are studying. It's not meant to sit on your shelf!

Remember: you are a very important figure for your learners. You are a living witness of the faith you seek to share with them. Your example speaks volumes. You never know when, through you, the Spirit will touch the hearts of your learners. God's grace works in mysterious ways. Even when you think a lesson may seem to be a complete failure, your kindness, your enthusiasm, your willingness to speak the truth, any or all of these, may make an impression on one or more of those you teach.

So, we hope you will make the most of this formation program. It has been prepared with much care, research, and prayer. May your "basic catechetical skills and attitudes" continue to grow by leaps and bounds.

So Great Our Hunger

Beyond the Moon and Stars

■ *Prayer is more about listening than speaking. Prepare yourself to listen by closing your eyes and concentrating on your breathing. When you feel ready, listen to the song "Beyond the Moon and Stars" (track 1 on the CD), ending with a moment of silence. Allow the music and the words to fill you.*

■ *Next, listen to the song again, but this time pay special attention to any words, images, or feelings the song evokes in you. When you finish listening, write these down in this book. You might also make note of any memories, hurts, or feelings you resist. Sometimes these are good indicators of how you block the Spirit from penetrating your heart.*

■ *Here are the lyrics of the song:*

Beyond the moon and stars, as deep as night,
So great our hunger, Lord, to see your light.
The sparrow finds her home beneath your wing, so may we come to rest where angels sing.

Our eyes have longed to see your loving face,
To live within your courts for all our days.

Upon our darkness, Lord, a light has shone.
You chose to dwell with us in flesh and bone.

When life's great journey ends, and day is done,
Then may our eyes behold your Holy One.

Song Notes

■ *When you're ready, continue by prayerfully reading the following reflection.*

Hunger

Hunger motivates us. In both the physical and spiritual realms, our energies are often focused on satisfying our hunger. St. Ignatius of Loyola understood this. In his handbook for spiritual growth called *Spiritual Exercises*, he invites us to prayerfully reflect on our deepest desires. What do I most want in life? What excites me? What are my hopes and dreams? In his wisdom, Ignatius knew that getting in touch with our deepest desires and longings is the key to finding where God is working in our lives.

Pause here to ask yourself: In the depths of my soul, what do I desire and hope for? Make some notes to yourself here.

Notes

■ ***Now continue the reflection...***

The Longing of the Soul

O God, you are my God, I seek you,
My soul thirsts for you;
My flesh faints for you,
as in a dry and weary land where
there is no water.
(Psalm 63)

While we certainly do experience moments of deep and profound happiness, we quickly realize that the satisfaction they bring is only temporary. Before we know it, we've moved on to the next dream, ever hoping that the next horizon will make us happy. We hunger for love, for intimacy, for belonging, for accomplishment, for peace, for justice, for the happiness of our children, for our first home, for a life-companion, for health, for wealth, and for security. While each of these may offer us temporary happiness, the satisfaction is always short-lived. We still hunger for something more.

Pause to reflect on your hunger. Ask yourself: How do I try to satisfy the longings of my soul? Where do I seek happiness? What do I seek that really doesn't satisfy my hunger?

Notes

Why do you think God loves the birds so well?

Often our answer reveals the areas of our life where we separate ourselves from God and where sin enters our lives. No one likes being hungry. Aching and in our hurry, we often look for satisfaction in things that ultimately are not good for us, and maybe even hurt us or the ones we love. Sometimes we turn to unhealthy relationships, addictive chemicals, food, sex, alcohol, or work because we are frantic to do something about this ache that exists at the core of our being. We hate it. It's not a comfortable feeling, and so we often run from it.

What St. Ignatius suggests at the beginning of his *Spiritual Exercises* is that we need to allow ourselves time to be with our hunger. Rather than running from it and trying not to feel it, we are invited to stay with our hunger and learn from it.

In God's Image

If we really believe that we are created in the image and likeness of God, we know that one of our most profound realities is that we hunger for fulfillment. Why? Is it because we long to return to the source of the superabundant love that created us? That nothing created ever totally satisfies our hunger? The entire story of salvation is about the unreserved love of God that constantly draws us into the intimacy and companionship for which we were created.

Who is your faith journey companion?

The ache that you and I experience deep in our souls was created by the One in whose image we are made. We are meant for God and God is meant for us. While we look for many ways to satisfy the hunger of our hearts, ultimately we will only find satisfaction in the heart of God. As St. Augustine tells us: "Our hearts are restless, Lord, until they rest in you."

Pause here and ask yourself: What thought or idea expressed in this reflection really stirs me? How would I repeat it in my own words? Take a few moments to collect and savor this reflection. Write down your thoughts.

Notes

Called to Give Myself

But if I am so needy myself, how can God possibly be suggesting that I offer guidance to other people on their journey of faith? If I am so hungry myself, how can I, as a catechist or teacher, help feed others? How dare I, weak and still on my own journey, attempt to lead others to Christ?

Yet we believe this is exactly what God is suggesting. Perhaps it's not so much about what we have to give—how much knowledge, spiritual wisdom, or profound faith—but about letting God use us as instruments. When we read the story in the Old Testament where God calls out to Isaiah in the night and bids him to go speak as a prophet to the people, Jeremiah can't believe it. "Me? You can't mean me. I don't have the words or the faith to speak such great things, Lord." And God tells him not to be afraid. "I will give you the words to speak."

Perhaps those to whom we are sent as catechists and teachers are not so much seeking answers as looking for a pilgrim companion, someone who is willing to walk alongside them on the journey of faith. No one else is able to provide the answer their hearts seek. But what you can offer is companionship in faith, willingness to journey with them, asking the questions of life, searching out the answers together, walking the path of death and resurrection with them as spiritual friends.

Faith-Filled Living

Perhaps the most helpful thing we can offer each other on this journey of faith is a willingness to let others know the hunger of our own hearts, to know our hopes and dreams, and to see how we try to live them out. By offering others a glimpse into our own journey of faith, we give the best guidance possible. When we teach from our weakness, without the arrogance of thinking we have the right answers, we offer the greatest gift. By this we make ourselves secondary to the movement of God's Spirit.

Our goal is not to get in the way of grace, but to open the door for grace.

The words that we use to teach are only symbols of what resides inside of us. They are meaningless if our lives—the way we live our faith—do not show what we speak. St. Ignatius proposes that love shows itself more perfectly in deeds than in words.

Love manifests itself in the mutual sharing
Of what we have,
And who we are,
With those we love.

Love shows itself more perfectly in deeds than in words.[1]

So, too, our faith-filled living speaks more loudly than any words we might speak about God or faith. Our words become meaningless if our lives do not live out the faith of which we speak. The greatest gift we can offer those who God gives us to guide is allowing them to see faith alive in us. This is what will make us great catechists and teachers. This is what God calls us to. At the end of life, having completed this mission with grace and faith will be what matters most.

[1] Author's paraphrase of #230–231 of *The Spiritual Exercises of St. Ignatius: A New Translation* by Louis Puhl, SJ, The Newman Press.

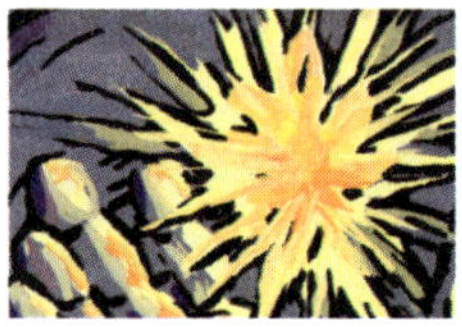  

The Time of Prayer

- ***Ignatius ends each of his exercises with a "colloquy," a heartfelt prayer, in one's own words, in the presence of God. It should be like a friend talking to a friend. Begin with the words below, and then continue to talk to God however your heart moves you. Stay with the prayer as long as it seems right to do so.***

- ***If you'd like to make notes to help you recall your time of prayer, you may do so in the space provided here.***

Ever faithful God,
open the doors of my heart.
Help me, O Lord,
to recognize the hunger you created in me,
to be aware of the deepest desires of my heart,
to know that I will find you in the midst of my longing.
Deepen my faith, dear God,
that I might walk in faith beside those you have entrusted to my care.

When you are ready, end by praying the Our Father.

The Growing Faith Project booklet for this session is #1.

1 The inborn hunger for God

Content summary of booklet #1

- *We are religious beings by nature.*
- *We are made to live in communion with God.*
- *Being with God is the only way to find happiness.*
- *When we listen to the message of creation and to the voice of conscience, we can arrive at certainty about the existence of God.*

This booklet makes reference to articles 26–49 in the *Catechism of the Catholic Church.*

Excerpt from booklet #1

The inborn hunger

The human heart is filled with hunger.
No matter who we are or where we live,
no matter how rich or poor we've become,
no matter to whom we're married,
or not married at all,
no matter what,
we hunger.
And for what is it that we humans hunger?
When we pause to consider this,
in all its magnitude and power,
we realize that we hunger for that One who made us.
We hunger for the divine heart.
We hunger for God.
This desire for God is written into our very hearts,
because we are created by God and for God
and God never ceases to draw us to God's own self.
Only in God will we ever find the truth and happiness
for which we never stop searching.

And even though we have
searched continually for God
down through the centuries
and even in our present day,
God, it turns out, is really quite near to us.
For in God, as Acts of the Apostles reminds us
in chapter 17, verse 28,
"we live and move and have our being."

Only in God will we ever find... happiness.

The Call to Be a Catechist or Teacher

Goal, Objectives, and Skill

The goal of *The Call to Be a Catechist or Teacher* is to help deepen your understanding of your calling, which means knowing and following Christ and leading others to him.

Your objectives are

- to better understand the nature of catechesis;
- to emphasize and teach that discipleship is the outcome you seek in catechesis;
- to take the catechumenate as a model for fuller initiation into the life of Christ and the Church.

Skill

- Sacrifice yourself as a catechist or teacher, working selflessly for your learners.

Preparation

- **Step One:** Experience the *Spiritual Exercises* for this session, and write reflections about your experience.
- **Step Two:** Read booklet #1 *What Does Your Heart Desire?* of the *Growing Faith Project* and do the reflections and exercises, recording your reflections.
- **Step Three:** Read the *Tools for Teaching* section carefully. It is important to articulate your reflections and applications in writing or verbally, whether alone or working as part of a group. If you are studying with a group, you will also enjoy the opportunity to share your experiences in learning sessions.

Step One: Setting the Tone

This optional section introduces you to a discussion of catechesis. Read the story on your own.

To Know Christ

A dialogue between a recent convert to Christ and an unbelieving friend developed like this.

"So you have been converted to Christ? Then you must know a great deal about him. Tell me, what country was he born in? How old was he when he died?"

"I don't know."

"How many sermons did he preach?"

"I don't know."

"You certainly know very little for a man who claims to be converted to Christ."

"You are right. But this much I do know. Three years ago I was a drunkard. I was in debt. My family was falling to pieces. But now I have given up drinking and am out of debt. Ours is a happy home. All this and more Christ has done for me. This much I know of Christ!"

To *really* know means to be transformed by what or whom one knows.

> The Christian faith is, above all, conversion to Jesus Christ.
> GDC 53

Step Two:
Importance of This Session

This section outlines and comments on the ways you can deepen your understanding of your calling. Read this on your own. If you take part in the group sessions, share your reflections with your group.

How can you grow in your knowledge and practice of your vocation as a catechist or teacher?

- Gain a better understanding of the nature of catechesis itself.
- Deepen appreciation of the principle that discipleship of Christ is the outcome we seek in catechesis.
- Take the catechumenate as a model for fuller initiation into the life of Christ and the Church.

God has loved us and called us to share that love as a catechist or teacher, to help others realize that they have a deep longing for God and will find happiness in returning that love. Our vocation as teacher or catechist is rooted in our baptism. We are ministers of the Word of God. We are specialists of the Word, direct witnesses to God's amazing action in human history.

Our baptismal consecration makes our proclamation and witness to Christian discipleship sacramental. In other words, our ministry is a living sign of Christ's presence. The Church commissions us to carry out this ministry in her name. When the parish community appoints or commissions us as teachers or catechists, it is the Church sending us forth to proclaim the Word.

As we fulfill our ministry, we are like instruments chosen by the Spirit to play the music of God's love for us in Jesus. When we grow in our prayer life, formation, and attentiveness to God and to our brothers and sisters, the music—the gospel message of conversion to Christ—that God wants to communicate through us will be as authentic and clear as possible.

Integrating What You Have Just Learned

- ***Reflect and discuss: What can you do to better understand your vocation and ministry? Write down your reflections and ideas.***

Notes

ON YOUR OWN

- *What does it mean to you to say your vocation is rooted in your baptism?*

Saints are people who let
the light shine through.

In this journey we are not alone. Just as the Church sends teachers and catechists forth for this ministry, so the Church is the setting for our ministry. Catechesis is a key element of the Church's pastoral activity. The word you live and proclaim, the sacraments you celebrate and teach belong to the life of the Church, the body of Christ of which you are a member.

Step Three: What Is Catechesis?

This session helps you reflect on the nature of catechesis. Read this on your own. If you take part in the group sessions, share your reflections with your group.

When the first disciples began to share the Good News, they proclaimed their experience of the person of Jesus Christ, living, healing, saving, teaching. Jesus revealed to each one the very life of God and God's plan for his people. Jesus didn't come just to *tell* us about God. He came to show us God, to put us in touch with God in his own person. That's the reality of the incarnation: that God walked with us, spoke with us, ate with us, dreamed with us in the person of Jesus. This loving plan of salvation revealed in the person of Jesus and handed on to the Church is the very heart of catechesis.

All catechesis includes much more than instruction (GDC 104). It is about a guided encounter with the *entire Christian life,* a journey toward ongoing conversion to Christ (GDC 105). As important as good content is, catechesis involves a lot more than content. Catechesis brings content to bear on our lives such that we celebrate our faith in prayer with the community of believers, such that our entire lives are converted to lifelong growing into discipleship of Christ, and such that we learn to share this conviction with all those who turn to us as we share faith with them. We are called to acquire the attitudes of Jesus, attitudes found in the gospels. We are to incarnate our faith daily, to become "living editions of the gospel" for our learners. All of this is nothing less than a gift of the Holy Spirit.

ON YOUR OWN

- *When did you first feel the call to be a catechist or teacher? Who or what was instrumental in helping you realize and follow that call?*

Integrating What You Have Just Learned

- ***Discuss with others in your group what catechesis means to you—not theoretically but practically. Reflect on your own experiences. Write down your reflections and ideas.***

Notes

Step Four: Discipleship

Your ministry is a sign of Christ's presence, a sign that you are a disciple of Christ. Read this on your own. If you take part in the group sessions, share your reflections with your group.

The definitive aim of catechesis is communion with Jesus Christ (*cf.* GDC 80). Teachers and catechists—as well as our learners—need to know him better, to know his mystery, to know the kingdom of Christ, and the "paths he has laid down for anyone who wishes to follow him."[1]

How is this communion with Christ realized? Jesus told his disciples, "I am the way, and the truth, and the life" (John 14:6). The way you will reach and teach others about union with Jesus is to accept him as your way, truth, and life, that is, to know, celebrate, and live the mystery of Jesus Christ, to die and rise with him, and to gradually lead your learners to do the same.

Your search for God takes you on a lifelong journey of discipleship. When you each say "yes" to Jesus, you hand your lives over to him and affirm your belief in what he has taught and continues to teach through the Church. You come to realize that you are not saved because of your own efforts but because of God's grace, which comes to you through Jesus and in the Church. And you recognize that discipleship has deepened your bond with the community of believers, the Church.

Means for Growth in Discipleship

What are some practical means for growing in discipleship and as a catechist or teacher? Read this on your own. If you take part in the group sessions, share your reflections with your group.

- On the spiritual level, develop union with Christ through an intense sacramental and prayer life, especially by celebrating as often as possible the sacraments of Eucharist and reconciliation. Pray Morning and Evening Prayer in union with the Church and meditate frequently on the Word of God. Foster Marian devotion and, whenever possible, participate in prayer groups and days of renewal or retreat. Having a spiritual director, a person trained to guide you along the path of prayer, is also very helpful.
- In daily living, engage in acts of faith, hope, and love for God and others, as well as honesty, integrity, perseverance, good judgment, openness of mind, and sensitivity.
- On the intellectual level, make the most of your catechist/teacher formation program to develop your understanding and experience of all the aspects of the Catholic faith and its practices and to learn ways for sharing this knowledge and experience with others.

Integrating What You Have Just Learned

- ***Talk with others in your group about your efforts at progressing in the journey of discipleship. What did or did not work for each of you? Or reflect on your own experience. Record your ideas and reflections.***

Notes

[1] *Catechesi Tradendae*, 20c.

tips

- Good teachers and catechists are always learning.
- An educator's knowledge of the subject is as important as the enthusiasm with which he or she shares it.

ON YOUR OWN

- *Where do you need to grow in your personal relationship with Jesus (for example, in prayer, in participation in the liturgy, in following Jesus' example of love, and so on)?*

Step Five:
The Catechumenate as Inspiration for Catechetical Ministry

The baptismal catechumenate provides inspiration for lifelong catechesis. Read this on your own. If you take part in the group sessions, share your reflections with your group.

We need patience with everyone
but first of all with ourselves.
St. Francis de Sales

The process of the catechumenate is a model for the initiation and ongoing faith formation of those being catechized in the life of Christ and of the Church. The baptismal catechumenate involves a journey. This journey involves passing through steps in which the catechumen first accepts the gospel and is signed with the cross, is buried, and ultimately rises to new life with Christ in the sacraments of initiation. Similarly, catechesis is for catechists, teachers, and learners a journey with Christ through his paschal mystery, ritually experienced in the celebration of the liturgy.

The word catechesis
has its roots
in the Greek word *katecheo*,
which means to resound or echo.

The catechumenate includes several rites and rituals, such as the signing with the cross, blessings, anointing, the Scrutinies, the presentations of the Creed and the Our Father. Catechumens break open the Word through a deep faith sharing that flows from their daily lives. Like the catechumenate, lifelong catechesis enables you and your learner to experience the Church's rites and symbols and unfolds their meaning. It provides ever deeper insight into the Scriptures and the faith of the Church through reflection, instruction, and formation. It draws you and your learners more deeply into the life of the faith community, especially in the Sunday Assembly. One of the vital aspects of liturgy is service, so ongoing catechesis encourages and motivates persons of all ages to acts of loving service to others, meeting the needs of the faith community as well as the larger community of the neighborhood, the country, and the world.

Catechesis aims to bring about
in the believer
an ever more mature faith
in Jesus Christ,
a deeper knowledge and love
of his person and message,
and a firm commitment
to follow him.

NDC 19A

Strategies for Making the Catechumenate Your Own Model

- Whatever season of the year you are in at this moment, try to enter more deeply into the spirit of that season: through reading and sharing of the Sunday readings; through traditional seasonal practices (if applicable); by observing the major feasts and solemnities of the season.
- Listen carefully to the homily at Sunday Mass and apply it to your own life.
- Use the Morning and Evening Prayer from the Liturgy of the Hours (there are simplified versions for those unable to pray the complete hours).
- Choose specific acts of service to carry out.
- Make an effort to know the other catechists or teachers on your team better. This will help build community and communion.

As You End This Session

During the coming week remember that you are called to be a "living edition of the gospel," and look for one or two ways you can put this into practice.

Integrating What You Have Just Learned

- ***Share with other members of your group your efforts in making the catechumenate your model in your own lifelong catechesis. If you are studying on your own, reflect on your own experiences. Afterward write about your difficulties and successes.***

Notes

ON YOUR OWN

- *Choose one of the signs, gestures, or rituals used at Mass (for example, the breaking of the bread, the sign of the cross, the sharing of communion). Then reflect on what it means to you.*

The Story of God in My Life

That Would Have Been Enough

■ ***Prepare yourself to listen to the song "Dayenu Litany" (track 2 on the CD) by closing your eyes and breathing deeply and slowly for a few moments. This helps to center you. When you feel ready, listen to the song, allowing for a few moments of silence afterward.***

■ ***Here are the lyrics of the song:***

If you had created us
and had not given us your light,
that would have been enough!
If you had given us your light and had not
made a covenant with your people,
that would have been enough!
That would have been enough!

If you had made a covenant with us
and had not called us by our name,
that would have been enough!
If you had called us by our name
and had not saved us from the flood,
that would have been enough!
That would have been enough!

If you had saved us from the flood
and had not loved us when we strayed,
that would have been enough!
If you had loved us when we strayed
and had not freed us from our slavery,
that would have been enough!
That would have been enough!

If you had freed us from our slavery
and had not led us to the promised land,
that would have been enough!
If you had led us to the promised land
and had not sent us holy prophets,
that would have been enough!
That would have been enough!

If you had sent us holy prophets
and had not promised us a savior,
that would have been enough!
If you had promised us a savior
and had not sent us your beloved Son,
that would have been enough!
That would have been enough!

■ ***Next, listen to the song again, but this time pay special attention to any words, images, or feelings the song evokes in you. When you are finished listening, write these down here.***

Song Notes

■ ***When you're ready, continue by prayerfully reading the following reflection.***

God's Generosity to Us

God is abundantly generous with us. We don't often take the time to reflect on all the ways God has blessed our lives, but that's the purpose of this exercise. We're going to pay special attention to God's bounty to us as we explore significant memories.

Begin by imagining God sitting beside you as you do this exercise. Together you're going to go through a photo album of your life. In this album are many memories—people, events, successes, failures, happiness, tragedy, and pain. These snapshots capture special memories in the story of your life and all of them together bring you to this day and this moment.

Each photograph from our memory album has a feeling attached to it. Sometimes the memories are happy ones, easy to stay with and embrace with peace. But sometimes the feelings these snapshots evoke will be painful, embarrassing, sad, or fearful. When you experience these difficult feelings, remember that God is there at your side. How did God guide you during these difficult moments of your life? Sometimes in looking back we will be able to recognize how God brought us to a new and better place.

We're not necessarily trying to search out long-forgotten or hidden memories, but perhaps you'll remember something that you haven't thought of in a long time. Take this as a sign that God may want you to discover something new and important. But most of the memories will be familiar ones because they are part of your often-told story. Whether the memory is familiar or foreign, look for God's guiding hand.

How has the hand of God been present in your life?

Take a moment now to recall your earliest memories and the memories of your early life. Look at the photos of this time. How do you feel about them? Can you find God in them? Write down what seems important.

Time Line

The Story of God's Love

Our photo albums are really not so much about us as they are about how much God loves us. True love yearns to reveal itself. If we take the time and look with the eyes of faith, each of the photos in our album are an example of God revealing love and care for us. God wants to tell us over and over again how much we are loved. Love expresses itself more perfectly in deeds than in words. The grace of this exercise is to allow ourselves to be overwhelmed by the love of God.

> *But God proves his love for us in that while we still were sinners Christ died for us.... Hope does not disappoint us, because God's love has been poured into our hearts through the Holy Spirit that has been given to us.* (Romans 5:5, 8)

God is in love with us. And so, like a good lover, he courts us and woos us with signs and symbols of love. When we don't get it, God tries again and again, all the while hoping that we will finally take notice. And God won't give up until we finally get the message. When we finally allow God to love us, the power of that love is transforming.

Now take some time to look at the photos of the middle of your life. Allow yourself to experience the feelings attached to these. Let God show you how he was present in these memories. When you're finished, write down some of the important ones.

Time Line

Unloved and Unnoticed

Many of us struggle all our lives to believe that we are lovable and have unique value. Sometimes we've been told in the depth of our soul that we are not lovable, that our life doesn't really make a difference. Who could really love me? If they really knew me, no one would find me lovable. If you struggle with these feelings, it is so important to ask God to open your heart to love. As you look at the photo album, let God love you.

God sees us just as we are, and yet loves us beyond words. God's love does not depend on our holiness or perfection. Even beyond that, there is nothing we can do to earn God's love. It is simply a freely-given, gracious gift.

God's love is
a gracious gift.

Now take some time to look at the photos of your most recent life. Again let God be with you as you do this. How was God present in each of these moments of your life? When you're finished, write down some of the important ones.

Notes

Seeing Ourselves with God's Eyes

What if we could see ourselves as God sees us? Are we not the apple-of-his-eye? What possibly could keep God from loving us? The truly amazing thing is that there is nothing at all, not even sin, that can keep God from loving us.

> *For I am convinced that neither death, nor life, nor angels, nor rulers, nor things present, nor things to come, nor powers, nor height, nor depth, nor anything else in all creation, will be able to separate us from the love of God in Christ Jesus our Lord.*
> (Romans 8:38–39)

The song for this exercise is based on an ancient Hebrew prayer that celebrates the abundance of God's love. We have been celebrating God's love as we've looked back over the photos and memories of our lives. Each time God revealed his love for us, it would have been enough. Yet over and over, God comes back to love again and again.

Take a few minutes to look back over the memories you have written down in this book and make them into your own "Dayenu Litany." Read each memory and follow it by adding the words "That would have been enough." The power of doing this lies in the progressive layering of the memories of your life. In each of them God has somehow revealed the depth of his love for you.

The Time of Prayer

- *Using one's imagination to pray is not pretending. St. Ignatius in his Spiritual Exercises often invites a person to use a form of imaginative prayer. It's a powerful way to use the mind and heart to connect with God.*

  For a few minutes close your eyes and imagine God's face before you. Let yourself see the features of his face. Look into his eyes. Let him look into your eyes. And finally, imagine God smiling as he looks at you. He is proud and takes great delight in you, his beloved one. Don't rush to move on. Let yourself bask in the loving gaze of God.

- *When you are finished, end with the following prayer or with a prayer in your own words.*

- *If you'd like to make notes to help you recall your time of prayer, you may do that in the space provided.*

Dear God, Lord of my life,
I sit in awe before the gaze of your love.
It is sometimes difficult to let you love me in this way.
I'm not used to its power and warmth.
But I want to let your love transform me
so that I can become a better disciple,
a better teacher and bearer of your Word.
Set me ablaze with the fire of that love.

When you're ready, end this prayertime by praying the Our Father.

The Growing Faith Project booklet for this session is #2.

2 God reveals a loving plan

Content summary of booklet #2

- *Out of love, God has revealed and given himself to us.*
- *God reveals the divine to us by gradually communicating God's own mystery in deeds and in words.*
- *God has communicated himself to us from the beginning of the human race.*
- *God has revealed himself fully through Jesus Christ, in whom God has established an eternal covenant.*

This booklet makes reference to articles 50–73 in the *Catechism of the Catholic Church.*

Excerpt from booklet #2

Where do you meet God?

God is Love...
Divine Love.
One cannot really see love with human eyes,
or hear it as such.
Yet using our own powers of observation,
reason,
and sound thinking,
we can come to know God.
We can be certain of the presence of Divine Love
because we can see the powerful outcome,
sometimes called "the works"
which God has done:
the creation of all the world
including us humans.
But we can also come to know Divine Love
because God has chosen to freely,
generously,
and lovingly
reveal the divine heart to us.

God has, in a word, given us a glimpse of mystery,
the divine plan of loving goodness,
formed and carried out down through history.
This divine plan culminated in Christ,
who is Love Revealed in all its marvelous fullness.
Through Christ all we need to know about God
was fully revealed.

Divine Love, by its very nature,
is communicative.
God wants to communicate the divine life to us,
the people God freely created.
This makes us all sons and daughters of God!
God wants us to be able to respond to the divine voice,
to know God's own heart,
and to love far beyond our natural capacity.

God has lovingly revealed the divine heart to us.

Preparing a Learning Space

Goal, Objectives, and Skill

The goal of *Preparing a Learning Space* is to help provide a sacred and welcoming environment for your learners.

Your objectives are

- to learn ways to prepare carefully and prayerfully before each session;
- to learn how to promote an atmosphere in which all the learners feel welcome;
- to learn how to organize the teaching space.

Skill

- Prepare a welcoming, organized space for learners.

Preparation

- **Step One:** Experience the material in the *Spiritual Exercises* and write your reflections.
- **Step Two:** Read booklet #2 *Where Do You Meet God?* of the *Growing Faith Project* and do the reflections and exercises, recording your reflections.
- **Step Three:** Read the *Tools for Teaching* section carefully. It is important to articulate your reflections and applications in writing or verbally, whether alone or working as part of a group. If you are studying with a group, take advantage of the opportunity to share your experiences in learning sessions.

Connecting Sessions

Last session you learned what it means to be a dedicated catechist. In this session you will focus on how to prepare a welcoming, organized teaching space for your learners, taking the Sunday Assembly as your model.

Step One: Setting the Tone

This optional section introduces you to the topic of making others feel welcome. Read this on your own.

Be faithful, then, in following the example of Jesus; be strong and firm in faith, and love the community as you love one another. Remain united in the truth and be as gentle as the Lord in dealing with one another, looking down on no one. If you can do good, do not hesitate, for charity frees us from death.[1]

[1] *Share the Light*, St. Polycarp, *Letter to the Philippians*.

Catechists are to identify and create "suitable conditions necessary for the Christian message to be sought and accepted."

NDC 54B.8

Step Two: Importance of This Session

Learning to make the space in which you teach or catechize a sacred, welcoming place helps your learners experience the presence of the parish community. Read this on your own. If you take part in the group sessions, share your reflections with your group.

How do you make your learning space a sacred space? Welcoming? Effective?

- Prepare yourself with prayer and become familiar with the content of the material you intend to share.
- Remember an experience of welcome in the parish community which you enjoyed. Consider why it was a welcoming experience, and incorporate that into your own efforts at welcoming your learners.
- Prepare your teaching space in a way that emphasizes your theme for that lesson.

Having a well-prepared learning space can pique the interest of the learners and invite them to participate in the sessions. Preparing or adding something related to the lesson to the meeting space or classroom will appeal to the imagination of your learners. Refer to your textbook manual for ideas. Have a focus object (something related to the lesson that will capture their attention), name tags they can create or that are already prepared, or some age-appropriate activity that will engage early arrivals. Keep in mind their age level—whether children, youth, high school students, or adults—in preparing your teaching space, and incorporate in some way a visible element of the liturgy.

Integrating What You Have Just Learned

- *Discuss with your group members the importance and value of preparing a welcoming teaching space. Reflect on your own experiences. What are some other elements you can use besides those mentioned?*
- *Discuss or reflect on the different kinds of focus objects or other introductory tools you have used. Which ones worked best? Describe the results of your reflections.*

Notes

tips

- Keep in mind the interests and needs of your learners in preparing the teaching space.
- Younger children like objects they can touch, smell, and so forth. Older learners, including adults, are stimulated by puzzles and objects that challenge them to think.

ON YOUR OWN

- *What makes you feel welcome when you attend an assembly or gathering? Why?*

Step Three: Preparing Yourself

You can learn from the word of God and the liturgy how to make your teaching space more welcoming. Read this on your own. If you take part in the group sessions, share your reflections with your group.

Love is the motivating force for your own preparation. In a sense you have made a covenant as God did with his prophets and his people: to proclaim God's word. In order to teach your learners about God, you will want to emulate God's teaching style. You can do this by reflecting on the word of God, by reflecting on the experience of gathering in the Sunday Assembly, by praying for your learners, and by knowing the content of the material well.

Strategies for Preparing Yourself

Refer to your catechist's or teacher's manual for specific suggestions for your lesson. Then read through these strategies.

- Use the Question of the Week to help you break open the Word from the Sunday liturgy and apply it to your life and your ministry. Whenever possible, do this with other catechists or teachers. The Question of the Week is a simple reflection question based on the Sunday gospel that is meant to be used by everyone in the parish as a means to share and grow in faith.

- In the Sunday Assembly, you gather with your faith community to celebrate God's love and your faith response. The welcome and unity of the assembly can be a model for welcoming your learners.

- Pray for yourself and your learners. You may want to keep a list of their names on hand so you can think of and pray for their needs as individuals, not just as a group.

- As the teacher or catechist, know the lesson well yourself. The lesson goes from your heart to the hearts of your learners. Know the major points you want them to learn, which activities to use and when you want to use them. Make the connection between liturgy and the lesson—whether through prayer or other means. Preparing yourself allows you to be clear about your focus—that is, the learners—to pace yourself, and to visualize yourself teaching. After all, your witness and enthusiasm is an important factor in teaching the lesson.

- Be prepared for the unexpected. Prepare alternate activities in case those you planned don't work out; have a "Plan B" in case a guest speaker doesn't show up, or your media equipment doesn't function properly, or for other unexpected circumstances.

Integrating What You Have Just Learned

- ***Discuss or reflect on your own:** How important is it to you to know your lesson well? What has been your experience in this regard? Can you contrast a time when preparation was done well with a time when it left a lot to be desired? Write down your reflections and ideas.*

Notes

ON YOUR OWN

- *What part does the word of God and prayer play in your personal preparation for teaching?*

Step Four: Making Learners Feel Welcome

Here are some ideas for making learners feel welcome. Read this on your own. If you take part in the group sessions, share your reflections with your group.

Hospitality and welcome go far beyond a simple greeting. In addition to the detail we give to preparing the learning space and creating a good learning environment, we also want to engage learners by name and to help them participate in creating a warm learning environment for their fellow learners. In the first gatherings, name tags are very important, not only helping people feel a sense of belonging, but also allowing them the freedom of engaging with others whom they may not know too well. As the entire group begins to address each other by name, the importance of each learner is implicitly affirmed, as well as their presence and their contribution to the group as a body. Appropriate sharing of our life's experiences fosters a culture of mutual trust and affirmation, which is especially vital to the adult learning experience.

Strategies for Creating a Welcoming Atmosphere

- Every learner, no matter what age, has different abilities and his or her own way of learning. Be alert to the need to affirm and honor cultural and individual diversity, and encourage the learners in expressions of their uniqueness. Point out that each of us brings different gifts to the Church, and so we add to God's family. We can all learn from one another. As we each bring unique gifts to the learning process, so too do we each have different styles and ways of learning.

- Create a learner-centered environment in which learners understand that they come before the planned session. Let them know that you give your time freely because you care about them and their growth as followers of Jesus. Show empathy. Try to see the world through their eyes. No matter what age you teach, talk to your learners at their

level. Show respect for their thoughts and recognize their insights. Help them express themselves if necessary. Never "put down" a learner or ridicule him or her.

- Draw out the learners who tend to be silent, but also challenge those who express themselves more freely. Show respect to both introverts and extroverts. Expect the best from all the learners, whatever their age. Stretch their minds and hearts through activities, questions, liturgical experiences, outreach programs, and so on. Keep communication open between you and each learner.

- Above all, share your joy in accompanying them on their faith journey. Present loving images of God and of Jesus. Show through your own example what the learner's relationship with God can be, especially as a part of your parish family.

Integrating What You Have Just Learned

- ***Share with others your experiences in making your learners feel welcome. Discuss what seemed to work best and why. Reflect on your own experiences. Write down your reflection and ideas.***

Notes

ON YOUR OWN

- *Do you know or remember what it is like not to feel welcome? Describe your feelings in writing. How can that experience help you as a catechist or teacher?*

Step Five: Make Your Teaching Space a Welcoming, Sacred Space

Arrange your space to create an environment where the learners can meet God. Read this on your own. If you take part in the group sessions, share your reflections with your group.

While most Catholic school teachers hold their lessons in classrooms, catechists have learned to teach in many different surroundings: a church, a meeting hall, a classroom, a living room, a church basement. The physical setup of your teaching space is important for "planting the seed" of God's word, for hearing God's word, but any environment can become a welcoming and sacred space if you keep these elements in mind.

> The catechist must consider all the human factors of a particular age level in order to present the Gospel message in a vital and compelling way.
>
> NDC 48

Strategies for Organizing Your Space

Through these activities, help your learners enter into the mystery of Jesus and celebrate his presence among us.

- Create a "prayer space" and let it be the central focus of your learning environment. The prayer space can be as simple as a corner with a few flowers and a Bible, a table covered with a cloth or a banner, a crucifix or other image according to the season, such as a Bible, a candle (be careful about fire codes), and so on. The prayer station will help make it clear that Jesus is the center of your lessons, of your whole program.
- Plan your seating arrangement. If at all possible, arrange the seats in a circle, semicircle, clusters, or some formation that allows you and the learners to more easily interact. (If you share the use of the room with another class, be sure to return the chairs to their proper places.) The seating arrangement also assists in managing behavior with younger learners and youth. You can separate talkative learners, place those who are "attention seekers" farther in back, and place learners who need more assistance closer to you.
- Make the room more attractive and functional by using pillows, small rugs, and plants. Have an activity center where learners can do alternate activities if they finish the group work early or where learners can process the lesson on their own.
- If you are a catechist and share your teaching space with others, bring objects and materials with you that relate to the lesson. Keep the materials together in a box, bag, or something else that is easily portable. Teachers may already have areas to keep their materials organized and at hand.

- You may often be able to obtain resources from local merchants: for example, large boxes from appliance stores; rug samples from carpet stores; paint and wallpaper samples from paint stores; brochures and maps from travel agencies.

- Visuals unrelated to your lesson are unnecessary and can prove to be very distracting for the learners. Use posters, pictures, decorations, and objects that relate to the goals of the lesson. Use the learners' own artwork as much as possible.

- It is always important to have the learning space prepared before learners arrive. Be there early enough to have the necessary time to prepare, so you can be present to the learners as they arrive. Have your supplies organized and any equipment you are using ready and in working order.

Do your best with the resources you have, then teach with confidence, joy, and love!

As You End This Session

Use your imagination in preparing your teaching space for your next session. Watch TV shows for ideas, especially if you teach children or youth. Refer to your text and other resources such as books and magazines for teachers and catechists. Ask another catechist, teacher, even your catechetical leader for ideas.

Integrating What You Have Just Learned

- *Map out the way you would like the learning space to look, bearing in mind the possibilities. Are there any changes you can make now? Which are the most important? If you are studying in a group, share your ideas with the others. Write down your reflections and ideas.*

Notes

tips

- Involve your learners in arranging the learning space.
- Don't conduct your lessons from a front desk or table. Use a small table, a lectern, or some other minor piece of furniture to hold your manual, your notes, and other materials.

Teach Me to Be Generous

Christ, Circle Round Us

■ *Find a quiet place. Center yourself by closing your eyes and breathing slowly and deeply for a few moments. Imagine that you are breathing in God's Spirit and breathing out all that is dark and dissonant. When you are ready, listen to the song "Christ, Circle Round Us" (track 3 on the CD) with your eyes closed. Allow for a moment of quiet at the end.*

■ *Now listen again. This time imagine God's Spirit all around you, circling and enfolding you. As you listen to the music, pay attention to any words, images, or feelings that the song suggests. Also pay attention to any feelings or memories you resist as you listen, since these sometimes point to ways that you may be resisting the working of God's Spirit. When you finish, take a few moments to write these down.*

■ ***Here are the lyrics of the song:***

Come, O Radiant Dawn,
splendor of the morning light.
Come, Sun of Justice,
turn away the pow'r of night.

Christ, circle round us.
Christ, may your light surround us.
Shine in our living.
Fill our hearts with great thanksgiving.

Come, O Flow'r of Love,
holy branch of Jesse's tree.
Come, Bough of Blessing,
bloom for all the world to see.

Come, O Gate of Hope,
holy door to heaven's throne.
Come, Key of David,
open wide the pathway home.

Come, Emmanuel,
cherished hope of Israel.
Come, live among us,
ever in our hearts to dwell.

Song Notes

In what ways are you God's work of art?

■ ***When you're ready to continue, prayerfully read the following reflection. There's no need to rush through. If there's anything that truly captures your attention, stay with it and savor it.***

God's Work of Art

Our God is amazingly generous and wants to give us everything with no limits. In fact, God desires our happiness more than we do. God wants us to know the kind of joy that comes only through intimacy. God wants us to grow in holiness and love. There's just one hitch. We've been given the gift of freedom and so we can refuse God. We can close our hearts to the work God desires to do in us. We can block the way to our becoming holy men and women.

At the beginning of his *Spiritual Exercises*, St. Ignatius encourages a person to pray for a generous heart. He understands how important it is to be receptive to God's grace. If we open ourselves, there is no end to the wonders God can and will do in us. God wants us to become holy men and women, and to become bearers of the Good News to others. God desires that we grow in faith so that we might become more effective catechists and teachers.

Growing in holiness is not our doing, but rather, God's work in us. People do not become saints because of how hard they have tried to be good, but because they have allowed God to take over their lives. We are God's work of art, and God is laboring in our souls to slowly but surely create something amazingly beautiful. When we are generous with God, he can mold us and fashion us into his holy people. Most of our job is just to stay out of the way and not put up walls that keep God out.

Take a moment to ask yourself: Do I want God in my life? Do I want God to change me? Am I afraid of that? What are some of the ways I resist God? Write a few words in the space provided that mirror your thoughts.

Notes

God's Generosity

When we explore the Old and New Testament scriptures, it becomes clear that the Holy One of Israel is very generous. First, there's the bounty of creation. Then there's the generous promise of the covenant with the people of Israel. Again and again God shows mercy on his people who repeatedly turn away from him and grumble when things aren't going right. God sends one prophet after another to speak to the people, to encourage them, to chide them, to remind them of God's care. And finally, God sends his own son, Jesus, to reveal the depth of his love.

No eye has seen, nor ear heard,
nor the human heart conceived,
what God has prepared
for those who love him.

1 Corinthians 2:9

God doesn't have to do any of this. There's nothing on our part that warrants such goodness and generosity. So why would God go so out of the way to shower us with kindness? Sometimes we get confused and think that we can somehow earn God's kindness. The Hebrew people thought that if they would scrupulously keep the commandments and carefully follow the prescribed religious practices, then God would take care of them and bless them with bounty. They believed God's love was dependent upon their goodness. They thought they could somehow win God's favor.

Reflect for a few moments on what motivates you to live your faith. Are there ways in which you try to earn God's love? When you're ready, write a few sentences about this.

Notes

Now continue with the reflection.

The God of Jesus

In his teaching, Jesus of Nazareth is very clear that God's love is a free gift. There is nothing we can do to earn God's favor. Living a holy, good life and doing good deeds does not make God love us more. Living a holy, faithful life is our response to God's overflowing generosity, not a means of earning God's love. It's about recognizing just how much we've been given and wanting to give God something in return.

It Isn't Fair

"But Mom, Andy got a bigger piece than I did!" protested his brother when given his serving of chocolate cake. "It's not fair!"

Are we not sometimes envious of God's generosity to those around us? We like to compare our lives with those of others. They can seem to have more than we do—more talent, more money, more love, more good fortune. It's not fair! Envy can poison our hearts and stand in the way of our relationship with God and others. We can go through life with a sense of entitlement. I deserve just as much cake as Andy got. But our envy blinds us to the truth of how much we've already been given. Everything we have is a gift, starting from the basic fact that we've been given the gift of life. Our envy can cause us to question the wisdom of God in dispensing his bounty as he sees fit. We are often arrogant enough to think that we'd know better how God's gifts should be distributed.

Please spend a few quiet minutes now to reflect. Ask yourself: How does envy show itself in my life? Am I angry with God because I think I deserve more? Do I judge God's wisdom? Write your words of reflection here.

Notes

The Time of Prayer

We now end our time of prayer with a prayer for the grace we desire from God. Today we ask for the grace of generosity of mind and heart so that we might be able to receive God's bounty. Begin with the words that follow, and then continue to talk to God in your own words.

There is space here to make any notes that might help you recall your experience of this exercise. Was it easy? Difficult? What seemed most important?

Thank you, dear Lord, for your overwhelming generosity.
You have been so good to me.
I want you in my life. Circle round me. Enfold me.
Break down my resistance to your love, gentle God,
and heal the envy of my heart.
Give me a generous spirit and in everything
help me to trust your love for me.

When you are ready, you may end by praying the Our Father.

The Growing Faith Project booklets for this session are #5 and #32.

5 Revelation and faith

Content summary of booklet #5

- *Faith is the personal loyalty of our whole being to God who reveals himself to us.*
- *In order to believe, we need the help and gifts of the Holy Spirit.*
- *Believing is a human act, conscious and free, corresponding to the dignity of the human person.*
- *Believing is also an ecclesial act. Our belief is stronger because the Church guides us and teaches us.*

This booklet makes reference to articles 142–184 in the *Catechism of the Catholic Church.*

32 Faith, hope, and love

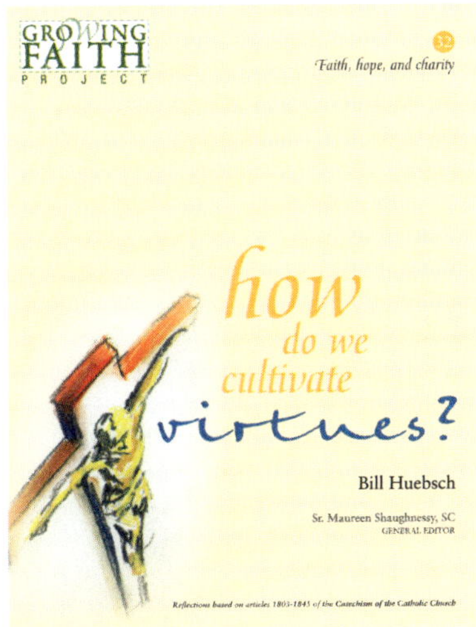

Content summary of booklet #32

- *Virtue is a habitual and firm disposition to do good.*
- *The three theological virtues are faith, hope, and charity. They inform all the moral virtues and give them life.*
- *Moral virtues can be grouped around the four cardinal virtues: prudence, justice, fortitude, and temperance.*
- *The seven gifts of the Holy Spirit are wisdom, understanding, counsel, fortitude, knowledge, piety, and awe of God's generous goodness.*

This booklet makes reference to articles 1803–1845 in the *Catechism of the Catholic Church.*

Excerpt from booklet #5

In whom do we believe?

We believe in God alone.
We trust in God
and in what God reveals to us through grace.
We believe in Jesus Christ,
God's Word made flesh,
the one who dwells among us.
And we believe in the Holy Spirit
in whom we find strength,
courage,
and the insight of faith.
Indeed, were it not for the Spirit,
we ourselves could not believe in the first place.
The Spirit reveals God to us
and only in God's Spirit
can we give ourselves over,
whole and entire,
intellect, will, heart, and soul,
in faith.

In order for us to believe, the Spirit prompts us in our hearts.

Planning the Learning Session

Goal, Objectives, and Skill

The goal of *Planning the Learning Session* is to highlight the importance of planning and preparing ahead for a lesson.

Your objectives are

- to learn how to set your goal and objectives;
- to learn how to plan effective lessons;
- to acquire different strategies for review and application.

Skill

- Plan lessons effectively.

Preparation

- **Step One:** Follow the material in the *Spiritual Exercises* and write a reflection on the experience.
- **Step Two:** Read booklets #5 *Do You Believe?* and #32 *How Do We Cultivate Virtues?* of the *Growing Faith Project* and do the reflections and exercises, recording your reflections.
- **Step Three:** Read the *Tools for Teaching* section carefully. It is important to articulate your reflections and applications in writing or verbally, whether alone or working as part of a group. If you are studying with a group, take advantage of the opportunity to share your experiences in learning sessions.

Connecting Sessions

In the last session you learned how to prepare a welcoming and organized teaching space for your learners. Now you will focus on another important preparatory skill: lesson planning.

Step One: Setting the Tone

This section introduces you to the subject of goals and objectives. Read on your own and do the brief suggested activity.

The goals and objectives for the learning experience are often outlined in the catechist's or teacher's manual. But what do they mean to you?

A goal is the main outcome toward which you work as a teacher or catechist. It is the primary *aim* of a lesson. Objectives describe *specifically* what knowledge and skills the learners will acquire by the end of the learning experience. The goal and objectives drive your lesson forward. Try to link everything you do in a lesson—presentation, activities, discussions, review—with one or more of the lesson's objectives and, ultimately, with the lesson's goal.

Formulate objectives that are specific, concrete, and measurable, keeping in mind the age, experience, and needs of your learners. For example, look at the goal and objectives for this session. As you read and experience the session, assess how well these objectives are presented and whether you attain them (at least to a degree).

> The effective presentation of the Christian faith also depends on the methodology employed in the transmission of the Good News.
>
> NDC 26

Step Two: Importance of This Session

This section outlines the key elements for a good lesson plan. Read this on your own. If you take part in the group sessions, share your reflections with your group.

How do you plan a lesson that is effective and engaging?

- Know your learners.
- Set your goal and objectives.
- Write lesson plans, including creative activities, that reach and motivate your learners.
- Acquire various strategies for review and application.

Well-prepared lessons are a skill and an art. Balance many elements to ensure that your learners are involved in acquiring the knowledge they need, learn how to apply it, and at the same time, enjoy learning.

Keep in mind that your learners are immersed in a culture in which people want to experience life directly, want to participate and interact, in which they look for images and hunger for connection. Your children, youth, and adults bring these expectations to their learning.[1]

Always try to maintain flexibility. Remain open to the Spirit and don't be afraid to change course somewhat if an important question or situation arises. Allow yourself sufficient time for planning your lesson. Above all, keep in mind the ultimate purpose of lesson planning: to lead your learners to conversion and commitment to Christ, and guiding them in their lifelong journey of faith.

Integrating What You Have Just Learned

- ***Discuss with your group members or reflect on your own: What do you find most difficult about preparing for sessions? Share ideas, difficulties, and suggestions. Write down your reflections.***

Notes

[1] John Roberto, *Becoming a Church of Lifelong Learners: The Generations of Faith Sourcebook*, Twenty-Third Publications.

ON YOUR OWN

- *Faith is passed on through both the witness of what we do and what we say. It is communicated in our lifestyle and our words. How do you make witnessing to the faith in your person a part of your lesson preparation? Write your reflections.*

Step Three: Effective Lesson Plans

This section describes the importance and major stages of good lesson planning. Read this on your own. If you take part in the group sessions, share your reflections with your group.

Lesson plans are important for several reasons.

- They challenge you to be prepared.
- They ensure that your learners absorb what they need to know.
- They address the individual needs of your learners.
- They help you make the best use of time.
- They afford a means to evaluate your teaching.

You have already learned the purpose of the goal and objectives of a lesson. The next step is to look at the three major stages of effective lesson planning:

- a stimulating opening
- the development of the lesson
- the summary and application.

We'll talk about the first two in Part Four, and the assimilation, review, and application in Part Five.

Integrating What You Have Just Learned

- *Discuss with the group your experiences in lesson planning. Or reflect on your own experiences. Share how you approach lesson planning. Write down your reflections and ideas.*

Notes

Step Four: Opening and Development of the Lesson

The opening and development of the lesson are critical in engaging and holding the learners' attention and presenting the message. Read this on your own. If you take part in the group sessions, share your reflections with your group.

Opening

A stimulating and engaging opening activity is critical to your lesson as the means to stimulate your learners' interest. Refer to your text and manual. Begin with prayer, followed by some form of activity that is age-appropriate and helps learners relate their life experience to the topic of the lesson. You may choose to use the Question of the Week to help learners break open the Word and share their faith.

After the opening, there are two more important steps. First, connect the present lesson with the last one. Such a review helps consolidate learning. Then briefly involve learners in an overview of the objectives of the present lesson, using questions, discussion, or an activity.

Development of the Lesson

The heart of the lesson lies in what and how the learners actually learn from the teacher or catechist. Refer to your catechist's or teacher's manual as well as the religion text as a starting point, but do not make these your only resources. Books, magazines, and other materials written for catechists and religion teachers provide concrete ideas and suggestions that you can put into practice.

Plan not only what to teach but the methods you will use to teach it. You want the lesson to "come alive" for your learners so they can experience the message and presence of Christ.

Strategies for Presenting the Topic

Vary your method of presentation using one or more of the means suggested here or others you have found effective. Refer also to your manual.

- Use the lecture format, in which you share information directly with the learners. Keep lectures brief, with a limited number of concepts, according to the age level of the learners. Lectures that call for the learners' participation or interaction provide a fuller learning experience.

- Use various forms of media, including music (especially contemporary scriptural and liturgical), film, photos, PowerPoint, or some combination of these to help you present the lesson. Prepare the learners beforehand and follow up with some form of discussion or conclusion.

- Brainstorming, conducting personal interviews and sharing the results, or having learners take part in an event or liturgical celebration (for example, a baptism) are all other methods of presenting and acquiring information.

- Activity centers that engage the different multiple intelligences (session 5) strengthen the message by allowing learners to process the information using their strongest form of intelligence.

Whichever method you choose for sharing the information, weave together the important elements of Scripture, doctrine, liturgy, and witness (Christian living).

Integrating What You Have Just Learned

- ***Which different methods of presentation have you used? Which worked best with your learners? Write down your ideas, successes, failures, and suggestions.***

Notes

tips

- When you prepare your lessons, visualize yourself teaching.

- Speak loudly and clearly while presenting the lesson.

ON YOUR OWN

- *Think about your own life. How do you learn best? What methods of teaching do you respond to?*

Sound catechetical resources in the hands of faithful and skilled catechists can be powerful instruments in the proclamation of the Gospel.

NDC 66

Step Five: Assimilation, Application, and Review

You will find a variety of methods for engaging the learners in active discovery. Read this on your own. If you take part in the group sessions, share your reflections with your group.

Methods

In addition to your presentation of the subject, you should utilize various methods for engaging the learners in active discovery. These methods must always serve a purpose, either to review, to assess how well the learners are absorbing the material, to help them assimilate and apply it, or all three.

Activities that help the learner synthesize the material

- Prepare age-appropriate questions that challenge the learner to think and to apply the lesson to life. Ask open-ended questions and questions that will involve them in discussion and/or require them to make decisions. Give them enough time to think about their answers.
- Faith-sharing, that is, sharing one's personal experience and response to a Scripture passage, world event, or story, is an effective means for growth as a Christian and emphasize the message of the lesson.
- Ask learners to integrate what they have learned by having them connect images with words, think of as many words as they can that relate to the central word, and so on.
- Engage the learners in small group work to discuss what they have learned and what it means to them. Give them the opportunity to explore the subject. (A great tool for this are the activities found in your text and manual.)

Activities that involve learners in hands-on actions

- Use hands-on activities or projects that allow the learners to create objects based on what they have learned, for example, mobiles, drawings, notebooks, posters, collages, murals, dioramas, newspapers, and more. These activities can be carried out by individuals or assigned to small groups.
- Involve young learners in movement: dancing, singing with gestures, games, processions, acting with puppets.
- Older children, youth, high school students, and adults can role play, prepare and act out stories, simulate real-life problem situations, take on creative music or video projects, be engaged in learning center activities, and take part in educational games such as a form of Bible trivia.

For every lesson, intentionally include a variety of different age-appropriate learning methods to enhance the learning experience. After the learners have experienced the subject matter, they will have the opportunity to pull together the information they have received and see it as a whole. In addition they will be able to use what they have learned in a creative way that engages not only their minds but their feelings and senses—the whole person—as well. Your choice of activities will therefore help them assimilate and apply the knowledge they have gained.

Review at different points during the lesson. Your learners' abilities to reason and apply material are more likely to be helped by questions such as "How does the sacrament of baptism affect your life today?" or by some form of activity.

At or near the end of the lesson, summarize the important points. Give the learners the opportunity to summarize also, through one of the types of activities noted above, that is, by synthesizing or by using what they have learned.

As You End This Session

Evaluate your last religion session. Think about how your preparation helped you.

Integrating What You Have Just Learned

- ***Share in your group the methods and activities you have used in your faith formation sessions. Reflect on your own experiences. Why did you choose them? Which worked best with your learners?***
- ***Do you evaluate your lessons after each session? Does your evaluation include not only the presentation but also how it affected the learners? Write down your ideas and reflections.***

Notes

tips

- A written lesson plan helps keep the lesson focused and flowing. It's also a valuable assessment tool.
- Invite as much response and feedback from your learners as time permits.

ON YOUR OWN

- *What was your own attitude during your last session? Enthusiastic, faith-filled, encouraging? Evaluate yourself: how did my preparation help me?*

The Beauty of God

For the Beauty

■ *Begin this exercise by finding a quiet place to be alone. Spend a few moments centering yourself. Close your eyes and breathe deeply. Imagine yourself breathing in the Spirit of God while you breathe out all that is harsh and dissonant. When you're ready, listen to the song "For the Beauty" (track 4 on the CD) with your eyes closed. Allow for a moment of quiet at the end.*

■ *Now listen to the song again. This time read the lyrics as they are sung. Pay attention to any words, images, or feelings that the song suggests. Also pay attention to any feelings or memories you resist as you listen, since these sometimes point to ways that we resist the working of God's Spirit within us. When you finish, take a few moments to write these down.*

■ ***Here are the lyrics of the song:***

For the beauty of the earth,
for the boundless skies,
For the love which from our birth
all around us lies,
For the blessings of thy bounty,
for thy gracious ways,
Lord of all to thee we sing
thankful hymns of praise.

For the beauty of each hour,
for the day and night,
Hill and valley, tree and flow'r,
moon and stars of light,
For the blessings of thy bounty,
for thy gracious ways,
Lord of all to thee we sing,
thankful hymns of praise.

For the joy of every love given on our way,
Friends on earth and friends above,
all who light our day,
For the blessings of thy bounty,
for thy gracious ways,
Lord of all to thee we sing
thankful hymns of praise.

Song Notes

When you're ready to continue, prayerfully read the following reflection. There's no need to rush through. If there's anything that captures your attention, don't hesitate to stay with it for awhile and savor it.

Beauty Opens the Way

Some have said that the experience of beauty is the forgotten key to open the soul to God. As teachers and catechists, we will often focus our efforts on imparting those truths of doctrine and those teachings of Christ that are central to our faith. While these may be important, they don't always lead our students to an experience of God. God remains at most a fascinating idea or a reasonable truth. One can talk forever about God, but until someone experiences the presence of God, they do not really "know" God.

Beauty is like a window into the divine. Just as the soul of any artist is revealed in the art they create, so too the soul of God, the Great Artist, is revealed in the world that is the work of his hands. If we take the time to see the beauty of this world with new eyes, we will be drawn into the heart of the Holy One.

Treasures of great beauty surround us, sometimes forgotten or overlooked as we hurry about our lives. They can be found in physical beauty, the vitality of youth and the wisdom of age, the mysteries of science, in acts of justice and forgiveness, moments of love and intimacy, and even in intense grief. Beauty is not always pretty. While it can be seen in the harmonious lines of a Michelangelo sculpture, it can also be found in the deep furrowed wrinkles of an old woman.

What and whom do you think God finds beautiful?

Take a moment now to reflect on the role of beauty in your life. ask yourself: How and where do I experience beauty? Do I allow beauty to be a part of my life? Write or sketch some of your reflections.

Notes & Drawings

Glimpse of God's Glory

■ ***When you've completed your writing, continue with the reflection.***

Hans Urs von Balthasar, one of the great Catholic theologians of the twentieth century, believed that the real starting point for a human encounter with God is an aesthetic experience of beauty, a brief glimpse of the glory of God manifest in nature or in a work of art. This experience takes us beyond ourselves, and into the realm of mystery and transcendence.

Von Balthasar urges us to read Scripture from a new perspective. He suggests that the word "glory," as used in the Old and New Testaments, is synonymous with "beauty." Here are some brief passages to help you experience what he is suggesting:

The heavens sing
the glory of God.

The heavens are telling the (beauty) of God;
and the firmament proclaims his handiwork.
(Psalm 19:1)

Long ago God spoke to our ancestors
in many and various ways by the prophets,
but in these last days he has spoken to us
by a Son,
whom he appointed heir of all things....
He is the reflection of God's (beauty)
and the exact imprint of God's very being.
(Hebrews 1:1–3)

Every valley shall be lifted up,
and every mountain and hill be made low....
Then the (beauty) of the Lord
shall be revealed,
and all people shall see it together.
(Isaiah 40:4-5)

Then an angel of the Lord stood before them,
and the (beauty) of the Lord
shone around them,
and they were terrified.
But the angel said to them,
"Do not be afraid; for see—
I am bringing you Good News
of great joy for all the people."
(Luke: 2:9–10)

An Act of Worship

Beauty has the power to transform the soul and instill gratitude as other things cannot. In truth, the experience of true beauty leads us to adoration, to worship. Pierre Teilhard de Chardin, the great Jesuit anthropologist and mystic, offers his own poetic voice in describing how beauty leads us to worship:

All around us, to right and left, in front and behind, above and below, we have only to go a little beyond the frontier of sensible appearances in order to see the divine welling up and showing through. But it is not only close to us, in front of us, that the divine presence has revealed itself. It has sprung up universally, and we find ourselves so surrounded and transfixed by it, that there is no room left to fall down and adore it, even within ourselves.

By means of all created things, without exception, the divine assails us, penetrates us, and molds us. We imagined it as distant and inaccessible, whereas in fact we live steeped in its burning layers....The world, this palpable world, which we were wont to treat with the boredom and disrespect with which we habitually regard places with no sacred association for us, is in truth a holy place, and we did not know it.[1]

(Teilhard de Chardin, SJ)

Take a moment to reflect on what steps you can take to surround yourself with beauty. Ask yourself: How can I bring more beauty into my daily life? How can I make the experience of beauty a part of my prayer? Write down your ideas or sketch them in the space provided here.

Notes & Drawings

How can you lead others to see beauty?

Teaching Others to See

We desperately need to experience beauty if we are to be people of hope. The world is so laden with brutality, greed, and selfishness; we need to stand against this darkness, and focus on the beauty of God's redeeming love. Perhaps our primary task as catechists and teachers is to help our students see this beauty around them, which is not always apparent and is sometimes hidden beneath the surface of things. We give them a priceless gift when we help them to be open to God's beauty, and experience it with wonder and adoration.

[1] Pierre Teilhard de Chardin, SJ. *The Divine Milieu*, New York: Harper & Row.

The Time of Prayer

■ ***Close your eyes and for a few moments picture something beautiful that you saw today. Stay with that image and take its goodness into your soul. You don't need to say anything. Just allow your heart to be moved to adoration of the Creator.***

When you're ready, continue with the following prayer, or with a prayer in your own words. Speak to God as the child of God that you are, with your heart fully open to him.

■ ***In the space below, write a few sentences to remind yourself of the graces of this time of prayer and reflection.***

Great and wonderful God,
I stand here in awe before this beauty you have created.
It is just one reflection of the goodness and beauty that is yours.
I ask for the grace to open my soul to the beauty that surrounds me,
often hiding beneath the surface of things,
sometimes missed because I am moving so fast.
There is so much brutality and ugliness in this world
and I need to be reminded
that there is goodness and beauty here too.

End by praying the Our Father when you are ready.

The Growing Faith Project booklets for this session are #21 and #22.

21 Liturgy, the work of the Trinity

Content summary of booklet #21

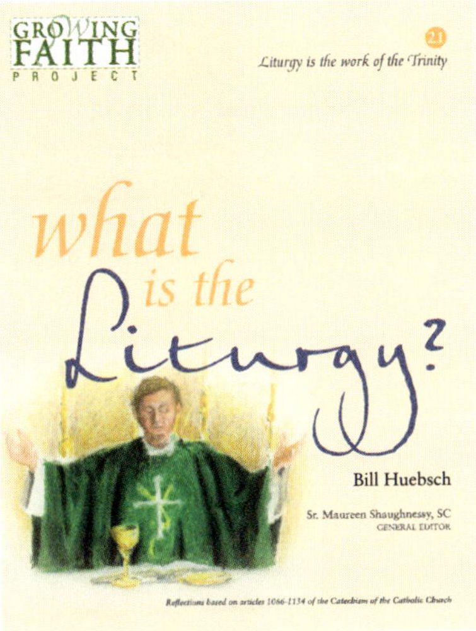

- *In the liturgy of the Church, God the Father is acknowledged and praised as the source of all the gifts of creation.*
- *Christ's work in the liturgy is sacramental. His body, the Church, is a sacrament through which the Holy Spirit dispenses the mystery of salvation.*
- *The Holy Spirit prepares the assembly to encounter Christ in the liturgy.*
- *The sacraments are signs of grace, instituted by Christ and entrusted to the Church.*

This booklet makes reference to articles 1066–1134 in the *Catechism of the Catholic Church*.

22 The celebration of the Liturgy

Content summary of booklet #22

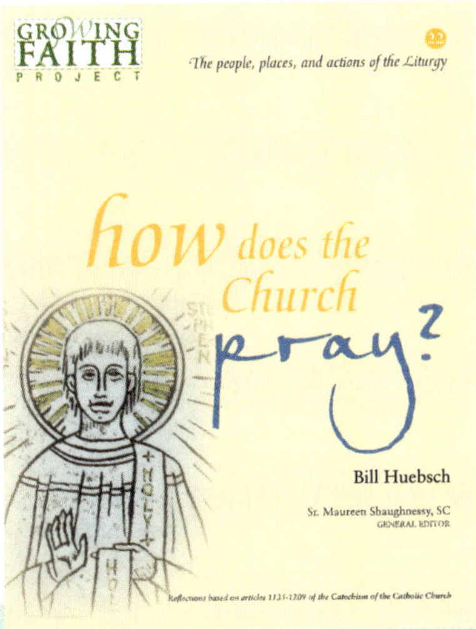

- *The Liturgy of the Word is an integral part of each liturgy celebrated by the Church.*
- *Sunday is the principal day for the celebration of the Eucharist because it is the day of the resurrection.*
- *The Church, "in the course of the year...unfolds the whole mystery of Christ."*
- *The diverse liturgical traditions or rites manifest the catholicity of the Church.*

This booklet makes reference to articles 1135–1209 in the *Catechism of the Catholic Church*.

Excerpt from booklet #21

Why the Liturgy?

Down through the centuries,
God prepared us through words and deeds among us
to be evermore ready to receive this gift:
the revelation of God.
In Christ, that work was completed
and for that reason,
we celebrate above all the Paschal Mystery
when we celebrate liturgy.

For us Christians it refers to our participation
in God's work,
the work of God in the world.
It is a reference to worship, yes,
but also to living as the Body of Christ,
proclaiming the Good News
and living in charity.

The liturgy provides a foretaste of heaven!

Liturgy as a Teaching Moment

Goal, Objectives, and Skill

The goal of *Liturgy as a Teaching Moment* is to help you connect liturgy with catechesis.

Your objectives are

- to learn how to break open the word of God together with your learners;
- to learn how to effectively integrate the liturgy into the formation session;
- to learn how to use the period of post-baptismal catechesis, or mystagogia, as a time to grow in the understanding of the liturgy.

Skill

- Live the liturgy so it will also be an important element of your teaching.

Preparation

- **Step One:** Reflect on the material in the *Spiritual Exercises* and write your reflections.
- **Step Two:** Read booklets #21 *What Is the Liturgy?* and #22 *How Does the Church Pray?* of the *Growing Faith Project* and do the reflections and exercises, recording your reflections.
- **Step Three:** Read the *Tools for Teaching* section carefully. It is important to articulate your reflections and applications in writing or verbally, whether alone or working as part of a group. If you are studying with a group, take advantage of the opportunity to share your experiences in learning sessions.

Connecting Sessions

In the last two sessions you learned how to organize a welcoming teaching space and how to plan lessons effectively. In this session you will be able to apply those skills while learning how to make liturgy an important element of your teaching.

Step One: Setting the Tone

This optional section introduces you to the topic of connecting liturgy and catechesis. Read and reflect on the passage from the *Jerusalem Catechesis*.

You were brought to the baptismal font just as Christ was taken down from the cross and placed in the tomb. Each of you was asked, "Do you believe in the name of the Father and of the Son and of the Holy Spirit?" You made the profession of faith that brings salvation, then you were immersed in the water and three times rose again. This is a symbol of the three days Christ spent in the tomb. When you were immersed in the water, it was as though night had fallen and you could not see in the darkness. But when you came out of the water, it was like coming into the light of day. At that moment you died and were born again. This is an amazing thing! We did not actually die and rise; we only did this symbolically. But we have truly been saved. We share in Christ's passion through symbols and gain salvation in reality. How boundless is Christ's love![1]

[1] Mystagogy V, from St. Cyril of Jerusalem: Catechesis (Jerusalem Catechesis).

Step Two:
Importance of This Session

Part two outlines ways of linking liturgy and catechesis. Read this on your own. If you take part in the group sessions, share your reflections with your group.

How do you assist learners in understanding the nature of the liturgy and how it unfolds in the Church?

- Break open the word of God together with your learners.
- Find ways to integrate the liturgy into your formation sessions
- Use mystagogy as a model for your catechesis.

In the liturgy we celebrate the paschal mystery of Christ. When we participate in the liturgy, we take part in the act of worship, but we also commit ourselves to living as the body of Christ, proclaiming the Good News of Jesus and living a life of love. Through the action of the Spirit, liturgy shapes our lives as Christians.

Catechesis and liturgy are closely linked. We can't just "learn about" the mystery of Christ and our faith, we also have to experience it, and we do this in the celebrations of the liturgy.

> Liturgical catechesis prepares for the sacraments by promoting a deeper understanding and experience of the liturgy.
>
> GDC 71

Integrating What You Have Just Learned

- ***Discuss with your group or reflect on your own on the importance of integrating liturgy with catechesis. What are some ways you have already done this? Have they been effective? Write down your reflections and ideas.***

Notes

ON YOUR OWN

- *What is your personal experience of participation in the liturgy? Be specific.*
- *In what areas do you feel you can improve? How?*

Step Three: Break Open the Word

This section presents Mary as the model for contemplating and applying the Word to her life. It describes how you can break open the Word with your learners. Read this on your own. If you take part in the group sessions, share your reflections with your group.

"While Mary contemplated everything she had read and heard, she grew even more in faith, wisdom, and charity. The mysteries of God were opened up to her, and joy filled her heart. Her mind was entirely blessed because, through the presence and action of the Spirit, she was always open to the power of God's word.

"Do as Mary did. Look deep into your heart so you can be cleansed from your sins."[1]

Jesus said, "But as for what was sown on good soil, this is the one who hears the word and understands it, who indeed bears fruit and yields, in one case a hundredfold, in another sixty, and in another thirty." (Mt 13:23)

tips

- Develop your familiarity with the Bible—its layout, the notes, and additional resources it contains for better understanding the Word.
- Develop an appreciation for the different styles of writing in the Bible.
- Don't be distracted or misled by literal interpretations of the Bible. In breaking open the Word, you are helping your learners.

[1] St. Lawrence Justinian, *Sermon on the Purification of the Blessed Virgin Mary.*

Breaking open the Word with your learners entails these steps.

- Read the Scripture passage together prayerfully, using a Bible adapted to their age.
- Ask your learners to listen with their hearts.
- Help the learners search for God's word for them and for the community of believers which they can apply to their lives. This is the key to the whole prayerful process. You can use the Question of the Week to help your learners share their faith.
- If necessary, guide them in reaching a decision to act on what they have shared.

Integrating What You Have Just Learned

Share with those in your group or reflect on your own: What part does listening play in breaking open the Word? What do you think it means to "listen with the heart"? What qualities do you need to truly listen to God and to one another? Write down your reflections and ideas.

Notes

Step Four: Linking Liturgy and Catechesis

Catechesis and liturgy are intimately connected. Read this on your own. If you take part in the group sessions, share your reflections with your group.

Catechesis is not just about learning truths; it's about experiencing the mystery of Christ, especially in the ritual activities of the Church. We call these rituals the Liturgy.

Catechesis prepares persons for the liturgy

- Prepare the learners for a full, conscious, and active participation in the mystery of the liturgy[2] by teaching them the meaning of the rites and symbols.

Catechesis flows naturally from good liturgy

- Emphasize the worship and honor of God.
- Help the learners engage the meaning of the rites and rituals of the liturgy.
- Help the learners reflect on their experience of the sacraments and the Sunday liturgy.
- Guide the learners in applying the meaning of the liturgy to their own lives, especially in the call to serve others.

Liturgy done well is itself living catechesis

- Review the whole history of salvation as it is celebrated in the sacraments, especially in the Sunday Eucharist through the cycle of the liturgical year. In the liturgy we come to know the living God.
- Discover how the truths of faith proclaimed in the Scriptures and the Creed shape your own faith and that of the learners.
- Discuss how the liturgy forms us in a life that is communal, always sending us out in service of our sisters and brothers.
- Employ the music used during the liturgy as another means of catechesis.

The Liturgical Year

The essential way in which we as Catholics link liturgy and catechesis is the celebration of the liturgical year. The liturgical year expresses and shapes our Christian identity. It is the celebration of Christ's life throughout the year.

- Follow the ministry, life, passion, death, and resurrection of Christ with the learners as we are immersed in it during the seasons of the Church year: Advent, Christmas, Epiphany, Lent, the Triduum, Easter, Pentecost, Ordinary Time.
- On the feast days, holy days, and solemnities, celebrate the mysteries of Jesus and the witness of persons who lived out the paschal mystery.

Linking liturgy and catechesis is about faith formation and transformation, conversion and discipleship.

[2] cf. *Constitution on the Sacred Liturgy*, 14.

Integrating What You Have Just Learned

- ***Discuss or reflect on how you celebrate the liturgical year in your faith formation sessions. Write about your experiences and ideas.***

Notes

tips

- Make a list of the learners' names and observe their saints' feast days in some way.
- Ask the learners to recall some part of the Sunday Mass from the previous week. Ask them to share how it touched them and why.

ON YOUR OWN

- *How do you observe the liturgical year in your own life?*

> In the broader sense, mystagogy represents the Christian's lifelong education and formation in the faith.
>
> NDC 35D

Step Five: Engaging in the Mystagogical Process in Catechesis

This section discusses mystagogy and its place in catechesis. Read this on your own. If you take part in the group sessions, share your reflections with your group.

"Mystagogy" means "guiding into mystery." The word most often refers to the final period of the process of Christian initiation for neophytes, those newly baptized at the Easter Vigil. During the Easter season they and the whole community enter more deeply into the mystery of God's love for us in Christ. Meditation on the Sunday readings and on their experience of the liturgy are two of the principal ways in which neophytes relate the Easter message and mystery to their lives and to their own stories of conversion and transformation. In turn the neophytes and the community grow in their awareness that as disciples of Jesus we are all called to proclaim God's kingdom.

The baptismal catechumenate and, in particular, the time of mystagogy emphasizes the need for lifelong catechesis. Because we are all in a sense continuing the time of mystagogy, that is post-baptismal catechesis, the elements of mystagogy that serve as a model for catechesis include:

- meditation on the Sunday gospel, especially through faith sharing;
- celebration of the Sunday Eucharist with the community;
- reflection on the experience of the sacraments;
- growth in communion with the members of the faith community;
- the study of Scripture and the liturgy;
- study of the social teachings of the Church;
- growth in prayer and acts of charity, especially in works of justice.

Strategies for Different Age Levels

According to their age level, help learners enter into mystery and understand it at least a little. Teach them about the liturgical year and what each season teaches us about Jesus and about God's love for us.

- Young learners absorb material well through movement, handling objects, singing, and so on. Involve primary age children in processions, such as placing the Bible on the prayer table before breaking open the Word. Use Bible stories, symbolic objects, liturgical music, gestures, and visuals to help them enter into the mystery of Jesus. Involve them in simple, hands-on seasonal activities.

- Intermediate-age children like to explore. After obtaining the necessary permissions, take the learners for a tour of the parish Church. Help them become familiar and comfortable with each space. Or have them experience a liturgy, and later revisit it by pointing out the various elements of the experience. Discuss the symbolism of the various liturgical colors.

- Middle-school learners like to work in small groups and to do research. For example, they might prepare banners for your parish Church or teaching space. They can look up the history of feasts, seasons, and traditions, as well as the development of the liturgy. Let them choose a project they are interested in.

- Invite youth, high school students, adults, and the participants in intergenerational gatherings to form groups as families and individuals. You might have them take part in faith sharing based on the Question of the Week and the Sunday gospel. Celebrate with them the holy days, solemnities, and particularly the Triduum in meaningful ways. Have them prepare prayer services or rituals for the various seasons. Arrange learning centers with liturgical themes.

As You End This Session

As you go through the week, carry the message of the Sunday gospel in your heart and reflect on it.

Integrating What You Have Just Learned

- ***Discuss with your group and reflect:** How can you create a sense of mystery in your learning spaces?*

- ***How can you make the symbols and gestures of faith more accessible to the learners? Write down your reflections and ideas.***

Notes

tips

- Make sure every session or gathering involves some experience of ritual.

- Become familiar with liturgical expressions and teach them to your learners.

- Begin the practice of blessing your learners at the end of your sessions.

ON YOUR OWN

- *How do you deepen your own understanding of the liturgy, and therefore of the mystery of Christ?*

- *How do you relate the liturgy to daily life?*

Found by Love

What is it that so divides our world?

So the Love of God

■ *Prepare yourself to listen by closing your eyes and concentrating on your breathing. When you feel ready, listen to the song "So the Love of God" (track 5 on the CD) with eyes closed and ending with a moment of silence. Allow the music and the words to fill you.*

■ *Here are the lyrics of the song:*

Broad and high, deep and wide,
so shall be the love of the Lord!
Always true, ever old and new,
so the love of God!

Once we were lost, orphans of night,
left but to wander, longing for the light.
Found by a love that would not let us go,
we are God's children, family forever.

Strong are the arms of your mercy
that have saved us from our sin.
Great is the gift of our growing,
of our knowing such a love.

Who could believe what you've given us
by loving us in our longing!
Even death cannot hold our hearts,
so great the might of your love!

■ *Next, listen to the song again and follow the lyrics. Pay special attention to those words, images, or feelings that stir your soul. Be sure to include any images or feelings that you resist. At the end, write these down.*

Song Notes

■ ***When you finish, continue by prayerfully reading the following reflection. If there's something in it that strikes you, stay with it and savor it.***

The Distortion of Beauty

Sin is not pretty and true evil is horrific. The reality of our world is that sin and evil exist alongside breathtaking goodness and beauty. We would much rather ignore the sin in our lives and anesthetize ourselves to the evil that surrounds us. The grace we seek in this exercise is to "own" the sadness, confusion, and shame that our sins cause. It is not easy to look evil squarely in the eye, to see it for exactly what it is. But we do this with God's strong, reassuring hand on our shoulder, ever reminding us of the power of saving mercy.

This whole world—every animal and human being, the wind and sea, the moon and stars—was created good and beautiful by God. Sin enters this world when we twist and distort that goodness and beauty into something it was never meant to be. For example, power can be used for tremendous good as well as for brutal acts of violence. The wonders of scientific knowledge can be used to save lives or destroy thousands. Terrible things are done every day in the name of love.

Take a moment now to read today's news from the newspaper or on the Internet. Awakened to the sin and the evil it causes, let your heart feel the day's events as fully as possible. Imagine what the day would be like if love prevailed. Write down your reflections and feelings in the space provided here.

Notes

Evil Is Real

Evil is not just an abstract concept used to describe bad things and bad people. It is a living reality, a power moving in this world and in our lives. We might refer to this power as Satan. St. Ignatius, ever the soldier, names evil the "Enemy." Naming evil is important to Ignatius because there is nothing the Enemy wants more than for us to ignore him or to think he doesn't exist. The Enemy we name can no longer have power over us.

All creation is a gift to us, good and beautiful beyond compare. But the Enemy distorts our thinking, convincing us that this gift is our right, to use and possess for our own selfish pleasure. The root of all sin is this irreverence for the gift of God. We show this irreverence in many ways: toward the resources of the earth, toward human life, toward our own bodies, toward the forces of nature. Imagine the measure of God's sadness when these gifts, given with such love, are treated with disrespect and dishonor.

Evil doesn't exist in just newspapers, television, or the Internet; it dwells within us. We ourselves contribute to the distortion of beauty and goodness, often showing our own irreverence for the gifts of God. Sometimes our sin becomes a pattern in our life, so habitualized that we become immune to its destructiveness.

Spend a few minutes looking into your soul. Allow yourself, in the presence of Christ on the cross, to look at the sin of your life. Ask yourself: How have I shown irreverence toward the goodness and beauty of creation? Where am I vulnerable to the tempting of the Evil Spirit? Then write down some of your reflections in the space provided.

Notes

What is the deeper meaning of the cross in your life?

Our Rejection of God's Love

God's mercy is infinite. The shameful death of Jesus on a cross proves that God will spare nothing when it comes to our salvation. But what if we don't want to be saved? John Kavanaugh, SJ, professor of philosophy, author, and homilist, writes about our human reaction in the face of God's tremendous mercy and love.

> *You see, God so loved us, even in our sinful poverty, as to become one with our own sinful condition, to die with us, like us, and for us. That's how valuable we humans are. That's how needed we are.*
>
> *And the two screaming rejections of such love are these:*
>
> *"No, I am not worth your death. I was not worth your life and love. I am not worth your efforts, your forgiveness, your suffering, your passion." This is the response we give when we are so overcome by our own sin that we think it is greater than God's creation, more lasting that God's love, and more compelling than God's beauty.*
>
> *And the second response is even more tragic:*
>
> *"Thanks, but no thanks. You see, I do not need your love. I do not need your suffering and your bleeding heart. I do not want your forgiveness and your redeeming labors. For I am a 'self-made' person. I did it on my own. I pulled myself up by my own bootstraps. The others may need your death, your love, but not me."*[1]

Reflect for a few moments on how you respond to God's mercy. Ask yourself: Can I let God love me? Do I think I'm worthy of God's love? How can I allow his saving love to change my heart? Write down your reflections.

Notes

[1] John F. Kavanaugh, SJ. *Faces of Poverty*, Orbis Books.

God's Response to Evil

What you have been asked to do in this exercise is not easy. It's hard to look at evil, to see it for what it really is. It should make us want to run in revulsion. But, like Jesus, we try not to flinch. We may try to not let the sin of the world and our own sin affect us. The grace of this week is to allow ourselves to feel the sadness and outrage, the shame and horror, that are the result of sin.

We look to Jesus to see how a child of God responds to evil. He does not lash out. He does not repay evil by creating more evil. Rather, Jesus takes the evil into himself, suffers the horror and sadness, and redeems our sin with love. Whenever we experience sin and evil, even our own, our best companion is Jesus the Risen One who shows us the wounds in his hands and feet, the marks of evil that have been transformed by God's most amazing love.

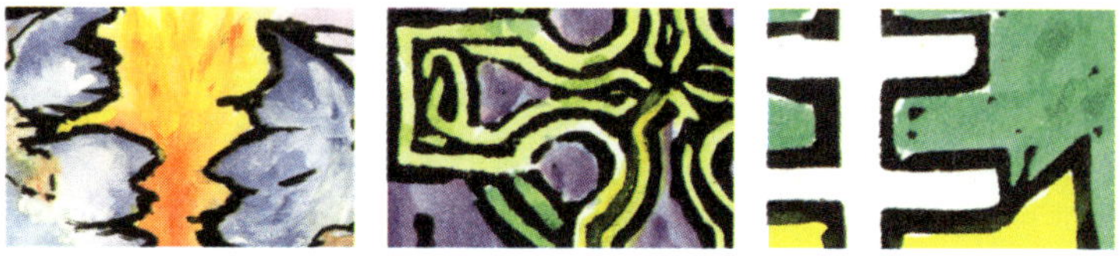

The Time of Prayer

■ *Close your eyes and for a few moments imagine yourself in the presence of Jesus, the Crucified Risen Lord. Let him show you the marks of his wounds. Speak to him about what is in your heart, in the following words, or better yet, in your own words.*

■ *In the space below, write a few sentences to remind yourself of the graces of this time of prayer and reflection.*

Dearest Savior,
I don't like to think of myself as a sinner.
I want to run from the evil I see in the world, to ignore it,
and even more, to run from the sin in my own life.
I don't understand how you can still love me,
and yet you do.
I see how you have embraced my sin, taken it upon yourself,
and redeemed it with a love that is beyond what I can fathom.
Please help me to allow the power of your love transform me.

End by praying the Our Father when you are ready.

The Growing Faith Project booklet for this session is #6.

6 The one true God

Content summary of booklet #6

- ***God is love.***
- ***God is neither male nor female. God is God.***
- ***God's name is YHWH, which means, I AM.***
- ***Faith helps us see and hear the truth.***

This booklet makes reference to articles 198–231 in the *Catechism of the Catholic Church.*

Excerpt from booklet #6

What is God like?

When we Christians recite our Creed,
we begin by affirming
that we believe in God.
Belief in God is the foundation of everything else
in which we profess our faith.
Our entire Creed is fundamentally about God
and even when we speak of ourselves
it is only in terms of our relationship with God.
Even the first commandment
begins with a declaration about God:
"I am the Lord, your God...."
We believe that there is only one God
and we aren't the first to believe this.
It's part of our ancient heritage of faith:
Even though we Christians speak of the Trinity,
we always mean to say that God,
the divine nature,
the divine essence,
the divine being,
is One.

And our belief in God is not based on fiction
or on wishful thinking
or on human invention.
It's based on God's own revelation to us.
In Deuteronomy we read what is perhaps
the most famous declaration of faith
ever written.
It's in chapter 6, verse 4:
"Hear, O Israel:
The Lord is our God,
the Lord alone."
This simple statement of belief
is the underpinning of all our faith.
Jesus himself quotes this line
in chapter 12, verse 29 of Mark's gospel.
When we profess faith in Jesus Christ,
and call him Lord,
or when we acclaim the Holy Spirit
as the Lord and Giver of Life,
we do not compromise our deep faith
in one God.
Indeed, we firmly profess
that we believe in one God.

We believe in one God.

Applying Principles of Development

Goal, Objectives, and Skill

The goal of *Applying Principles of Development* is for you to learn about the nature of learning and the principles of developmental theory and multiple intelligences as applied to effective religious education.

Your objectives are

- to learn how to apply the principles of learning to faith formation;
- to acquire various methods to reach each learner;
- to learn how to apply the multiple intelligences approach.

Skill

- Recognize the ongoing development of each learner and use methods suited to each one.

Preparation

- **Step One:** Experience the material in the *Spiritual Exercises* and write your reflections.
- **Step Two:** Read booklet #6 *In Whom Do You Believe?* of the *Growing Faith Project* and do the reflections and exercises, recording your reflections.
- **Step Three:** Read the *Tools for Teaching* section carefully. It is important to articulate your reflections and applications in writing or verbally, whether alone or working as part of a group. If you are studying with a group, take advantage of the opportunity to share your experiences in learning sessions.

Connecting Sessions

In the last session we learned ways to make liturgy an important element of our learning sessions. Now we will learn some principles of learning development and how to teach about the liturgy—or any subject—using methods suited to our learners.

Step One: Setting the Tone

This optional section introduces you to the different ways learners learn. Read and reflect on these questions.

How do you learn best?

- By listening to an explanation?
- By seeing a demonstration?
- By doing the task or acquiring the skill on your own?
- By reflecting on the meaning of the lesson?

Step Two: Importance of This Session

This section introduces the various principles of human learning. Read this on your own. If you take part in the group session, share your reflections with the group.

How do you help learners move from knowing *about* Christ to an experience of an encounter *with* Christ?

- Apply the principles of learning to faith formation.
- Apply the multiple intelligences approach—different styles of learning—to faith formation.
- Use various methods to reach each learner.

The core of the human person is mystery. You as catechist or teacher are privileged to encounter that mystery, to encourage and assist in the growth of the person, to help learners make the most of their God-given potential to become persons of faith and holiness of life.

Learning has three dimensions: knowing, relating, and doing. Very young children are anxious to learn about things; they want to know. But they aren't able to relate one fact to another. As learners grow and develop, they move from just *knowing* about something to *relating* to that truth or relating it to other truths. When children reach a certain age they begin to act on what they know, that is, they *do* something with the truth they learn. When persons move through youth into adulthood their motivation to learn and their choices become, in general, less self-centered, and they are also moved to act for others.

When the dimensions of learning are applied to learning about Christ, learners first encounter Christ. They learn about him, hear stories from the gospel, and experience him in the liturgy and the Church. Gradually they move on to build a relationship with Christ, whom they have come to know. Hopefully they then choose to follow Christ and carry on his mission.

> The age and the intellectual development of Christians, their degree of ecclesial and spiritual maturity, and many other personal circumstances must be carefully considered in choosing appropriate methodologies.
>
> NDC 29

Integrating What You Have Just Learned

■ ***Reflect on and discuss:** In today's culture, the emphasis is more on learning through experience and within a group. Give an example of a topic you have taught using experience rather than explanation, for example, an aspect of the liturgy or the works of mercy. Write down your reflections and ideas.*

Notes

tips

- Knowing how the learners learn is just as important as knowing what they need to learn.
- Be open-minded to new ideas and new possibilities.

ON YOUR OWN

■ *When you are learning something new, consider what role your own personal experience plays.*

Step Three:
Grace Builds on Nature

The faith development of learners parallels the levels of human learning. Read this on your own. If you take part in the group sessions, share your reflections with your group.

Christian educator and scholar James Fowler, having studied the research of Jean Piaget and others, began studying faith development, which parallels the levels of learning. Some simplified points from his works are offered here.[1]

Children ages two to six or seven

- These children begin to develop what Fowler calls intuitive faith. The first conscious and concrete images of God form during these early years.
- Imagination plays a great part in their faith development, as does imitation of adults.
- Faith stories can help shape their beliefs and values.
- Concrete symbols, gestures, and rituals help form their understanding of God, even at an unconscious level.

[1] The works of James Fowler include *Faith Development and Pastoral Care*, Fortress Press; *Stages of Faith*, Harper & Row; *Weaving, the New Creation; Stages of Faith and the Public Church*, Harper Collins.

Children ages six or seven to eleven

- Story plays an important role in their faith development. They not only enjoy hearing stories; they like to tell stories, which become a way of expressing what they feel and experience and what meaning they give to their experiences.
- Their thinking becomes more literal. They want to know what is really true.
- They can see that the viewpoint of other people is like or unlike theirs, especially of people they know best.
- Children at this stage are very concerned about what is fair. Their view of God is most often that of a parent or other caregiver who is loving and forgiving but also fair, and who rewards good behavior and punishes bad.

Pre-adolescents and adolescents

- These young people have the potential for abstract thought and can reflect more deeply on the meaning of their faith stories and beliefs.
- Relationships with others, especially their peers, become more and more important to them. The desire for relationships is often extended to God, so as their faith forms, teens feel a longing for a personal relationship with God and a desire to please God.
- As they grow more aware of what others think of them, they seek to meet others' expectations.
- At this stage they develop the capability for discipleship and later for stewardship.

Young adults and adults

- They desire genuine spiritual experiences and answers to their questions about God and life in a language that speaks to their reality.
- They look for ways to serve others and to work for justice.
- They want to have connection with a community.
- They seek guidance in making decisions, especially important life decisions.

Integrating What You Have Just Learned

■ ***Reflect and discuss, or read on your own:*** *What are some ways you can build on the characteristics of the faith development of your learners? Write down your reflections and ideas.*

Notes

Step Four: Strategies for Applying the Principles of Development

How can you integrate into your formation sessions your understanding of the faith development of your learners? Read this on your own. If you take part in the group sessions, share your reflections with your group.

- Know the learners you teach, that is, their needs, their wants, their abilities, their weaknesses. See them as individuals, not just as a group. Find ways to meet their needs, build on their abilities, and strengthen their weaknesses.
- Reflect on the stages of faith development described by Fowler. (You may wish to do further reading on them.) Let these help you understand the way learners grasp material, how they make decisions, and how they relate to others.
- Read carefully the section in NDC 48 that applies to the learners you teach. The *National Directory for Catechesis* provides reflections on the readiness of different age levels and outlines the recommended approach, content, and methodology for each age group.
- Keep in mind the principles of development when you plan your learning experiences, choose your method, or prepare activities that are not in the text or in the catechist's or teacher's manuals.

ON YOUR OWN

■ *What did you learn from this session? How does this enrich your formation as a catechist or teacher?*

Step Five: Using Multiple Intelligences

The theory of multiple intelligences describes the ways different learners absorb ideas. Read this on your own. If you take part in the group sessions, share your reflections with the group.

Believing that IQ testing is very limited as a measure of intelligence, Professor Howard Gardner of Harvard University began to do scientific research on the ways people learn. He discovered several intelligences, centered in different parts of the brain but interconnected.

One way of approaching a brief study of these intelligences is to see how our Catholic liturgy engages each of them and how we can use them in our religious education sessions.[1]

- The *verbal-linguistic intelligence* is the most familiar and also the most obvious with regard to the liturgy. The Scripture readings paint wonderful word pictures and offer timeless stories that capture the interest of all word-lovers. Learners with this intelligence might rewrite or retell a story, be part of a story, report on a story, pray with a Scripture passage, and so on.

> Individuals develop as human beings and faithful followers of Christ in different ways and according to their own pace.
>
> NDC 48

- Learners with *logical-mathematical intelligence* are not only concerned with numbers but also with patterns and logical reasoning. They can be engaged by the logical patterns in the rituals of the liturgy, by the prayers that record the history of salvation, and so on. Activities that build on these elements may be used to enhance their experience of the liturgy and their faith.

- Learners with strong *musical-rhythmic intelligence* can absorb truth through the music used in the liturgy. They also learn through the beauty and rhythm of the words and other sounds as well as the silence that are part of the celebration.

- *Visual-spatial learners* will be attracted by the symbols and gestures used in the liturgy: the bread and wine, the cross, the water, the incense, the sign of peace, as well as the colors used for the liturgical seasons. Use these symbols in your prayer time, and discuss the deeper meaning of these symbols and gestures.

- Learners whose strength is *bodily-kinesthetic intelligence* absorb knowledge especially through movement and their senses. They will become involved in the gestures, postures, smells, and ritual movement of the liturgy.

- A strong *naturalist intelligence* gives the learner a sense of the order and purpose in nature, in their environment, as well as in worship. These learners can appreciate Scripture readings that speak of nature and of the order in the world. They also absorb knowledge through the structure and order of the rituals in our liturgies.

[1] See Bernadette Stankard, *How Each Child Learns: Using Multiple Intelligence in Faith Formation*, Twenty-Third Publications.

- Being quiet and reflective are characteristics of *intrapersonal intelligence*. These learners internalize what they see and hear. They are able to get inside a Scripture story and look at the reasons for various actions. Use activities that encourage learners to examine their experiences and relationship with God.

- Learners with strong *interpersonal intelligence* learn most from the community aspect of the liturgy. Worshiping with their families, friends, and other people has a strong influence on them. They also enjoy sharing the stories of others; again the Liturgy of the Word is a key element for them. Group work, teamwork, and learning about one another are important activities for these learners.

- Finally there are the learners whose strength is *existential intelligence*. They ask and tackle the big questions: the meaning of life, death, what is evil, who is God. The liturgy, especially the Liturgy of the Word, is all about the big questions. It challenges the learners to grow in their faith. And it comforts them. Prayer rituals, journaling, activities that give these learners time to explore the questions and God's plan for their lives are ways to engage and challenge their intelligence.

Always remember that sharing faith is a work of the Spirit. As catechists and teachers we rely on the grace of God to bring to fruit the seeds we plant in the lives of the learners. Build on the liturgical experiences of the learners in planning, and attend to their experiences of faith as they share them.

As You End This Session

During this week pray to know your learners better.

Integrating What You Have Just Learned

- ***Reflect on and discuss:*** *Share ways that you might apply (or already have) the multiple intelligences approach in your catechesis. Were your efforts successful? Explain. Write your reflections and ideas.*

Notes

ON YOUR OWN

- *Which form of intelligence best describes the way you learn? How have you used it in teaching and in enriching your participation in the liturgy?*

Nothing Is Impossible for God

Freedom to Say "Yes"

In this exercise we begin to use a kind of prayer that St. Ignatius in his Spiritual Exercises calls "contemplation." You may not be familiar with this kind of prayer, but it is very easy. Using the power of imagination, we enter a Scripture passage, not only to understand it, but beyond that, to actually experience it in our own hearts. This kind of prayer takes the story beyond its surface details and lets it come alive for us. We become participants in it.

Don't worry if this prayer of contemplation feels awkward at first. It may take some practice before it begins to feel natural and comfortable. If you feel self-conscious at first, that's OK. Stay with it. Focus on opening your imagination and heart and it will expose new depths of Scripture to you. It will also change your relationship with God.

First, find a quiet place and put yourself in the presence of God. You've already been doing this at the beginning of each of the previous exercises.

Begin by asking God for the grace you desire. In this exercise it might be the grace to trust God's love enough to surrender your life into his hands.

Next, read the Scripture text slowly through once.

In the sixth month the angel Gabriel was sent by God to a town in Galilee called Nazareth, to a virgin engaged to a man whose name was Joseph, of the house of David. The virgin's name was Mary. And he came to her and said, "Greetings, favored one! The Lord is with you." But she was much perplexed by his words and pondered what sort of greeting this might be.

The angel said to her, "Do not be afraid, Mary, for you have found favor with God. And now, you will conceive in your womb and bear a son, and you will name him Jesus. He will be great, and will be called the Son of the Most High, and the Lord God will give to him the throne of his ancestor David. He will reign over the house of Jacob forever, and of his kingdom there will be no end."

Mary said to the angel, "How can this be, since I am a virgin?" The angel said to her, "The Holy Spirit will come upon you, and the power of the Most High will overshadow you; therefore the child to be born will be holy; he will be called the Son of God. And now, your relative Elizabeth in her old age has also conceived a son; and this is the sixth month for her who was said to be barren. For nothing will be impossible with God."

Then Mary said, "Here am I, the servant of the Lord; let it be with me according to your word." Then the angel departed from her. (Luke 1:26–38)

How have you said "yes" to God?

Now put the text down, perhaps close your eyes, and use your imagination to picture the scene with as much detail as you can. Where is it taking place? Look around to see what things look like. Who is there? Picture the young Mary of Nazareth. What do her clothes look like? Notice the expression on her face. What is she doing? How does the angel Gabriel come to her? What does his face look like? Listen to their voices. Place yourself in the scene, either as one of the principle characters or simply as a bystander. Begin to hear what's being said and watch the faces as the events unfold. Let the story proceed however your imagination takes you. The details of the text will cease to be important. If a particular moment seems significant, stay with it and savor it. Most of all let your heart feel what's going on. Take your time. Try to spend 30-45 minutes with this part.

When you've finished, take a couple minutes to write down a few sentences about your experience. Did you find this part easy or difficult? What did you discover? Were you able to experience the story in a new way? What was most important to you?

Notes

■ ***When you're ready to continue, read over the following short reflection.***

How Can This Be?

Angels just don't appear to people every day, even in Scripture. No matter what form the angel Gabriel took, Mary must have been shocked and more than a little afraid. "You're telling me what? That I'm going to have a son? Listen. Maybe you don't understand. I'm still a virgin." But that doesn't stop the angel from delivering his amazing message. "The power of God's Spirit will do this." Perhaps there's a bit of sarcasm in Mary's voice as she replies, "Oh. OK. Now I understand. I've heard of several virgins who've conceived a child by God's hand." Imagine the twinkle in her eye as she watches the angel's face. "And by the way," continues Gabriel, "your barren cousin Elizabeth is going to have a child too. Nothing is impossible for God."

Nothing is impossible. All her life Mary had believed that God loved her. Here she was being told impossible things and being asked to trust in that love in a way she never imagined. Love stretches us sometimes and invites us to move beyond what is safe and secure. Mary surely didn't understand what it all meant, and she was surely afraid of what the future might bring, but her response comes from her deepest soul. "My wonderful God, of course I trust you. And I surrender my future to you. If this is what you want, let it be done."

Such surrender is really the basic decision of our spiritual life. Will I trust God or not? Will I surrender my life to God or will I choose to believe that I know better what is best for me?

Spend a few moments with this question. Do you trust God's love enough to surrender your life? What keeps you from giving your heart to God? Write down your reflections.

Notes

When you're ready, continue with the reflection.

Holy Indifference

Mary, the young woman of Nazareth, possessed a virtue that St. Ignatius highly values and admires. In order to surrender to God's invitation, our soul must be free, or, as Ignatius calls it, indifferent, whether that be to poverty or riches, sickness or health, long life or short, honor or disgrace. Most of us would much rather control the outcome of our lives than to journey in holy freedom, simply trusting that God's love is enough.

The Closing Prayer

This week the music will draw our exercise to a close. It is a prayer that we may grow in this holy freedom that enables us to surrender our lives to God. As you listen to the song "Come, O Lord" (track 6 on the CD), make it your own personal prayer. Allow for a few moments of silence at the end.

When and where has God asked you to stretch yourself and move beyond what is safe?

Here are the lyrics of the song:

Come, O Lord, and set us free!
God our Savior, set us free!

Show me the pathway for my life,
that I may journey in your truth.
I long to live within your gates,
in your presence, O God.

How kind and gracious is the Lord,
whose tender mercy does not end,
Who does not dwell upon our sin,
but redeems us with love.

My eyes are ever on the Lord,
whose love is steadfast to the end.
I place my hope upon the Lord
who is steadfast in love.

Song Notes

The Time of Prayer

■ *Now close this time of prayer by speaking to God using the prayer given here, or, better yet, in your own words.*

■ *The grace of contemplation is deepened when we take the images and persons of our prayer with us into our daily lives. So, as you go through your week, remember Mary and what you experienced in your time of prayer. Let the words and images be with you as you work, play, study, eat, and pray. As another means of bringing this exercise into your life, listen to the song during the week. Take it with you in the car, play it as you work around the house or before you go to bed. The grace of God will follow you throughout your week.*

Thank you, my great and wonderful God,
for teaching me so gently of your love.
It never occurred to me that Mary would have struggled
with the angel's message,
and that she might have been afraid and confused.
Yet I watch her respond so generously to you
and surrender her life to you.
Dear Lord, help me grow in holy freedom
so that I might give myself to you as Mary does.
Help me to say "yes."

When you're ready, end by praying the Our Father.

The Growing Faith Project booklets for this session are #3 and #4.

3 Divine Revelation

Content summary of booklet #3

- *What Christ entrusted to the apostles, they in turn handed on to all generations through their preaching and writing, under the inspiration of the Holy Spirit.*
- *Sacred Tradition and Sacred Scripture form a single sacred statement of the word of God.*
- *The pilgrim Church contemplates God, the source of all her riches.*
- *The Church, in her doctrine, life, and worship, passes on to all of us everything she believes.*

This booklet makes reference to articles 74–100 in the *Catechism of the Catholic Church.*

4 Scripture Is the Word of God

Content summary of booklet #4

- *God is the author of Sacred Scripture because God inspired its human authors.*
- *Interpretation of Scripture must be attentive above all to what God wants to reveal through the writings of the sacred authors.*
- *The Church accepts and venerates as inspired the forty-six books of the Old Testament and the twenty-seven books of the New Testament.*
- *The four gospels occupy a central place because Christ Jesus is their center.*

This booklet makes reference to articles 101–141 in the *Catechism of the Catholic Church.*

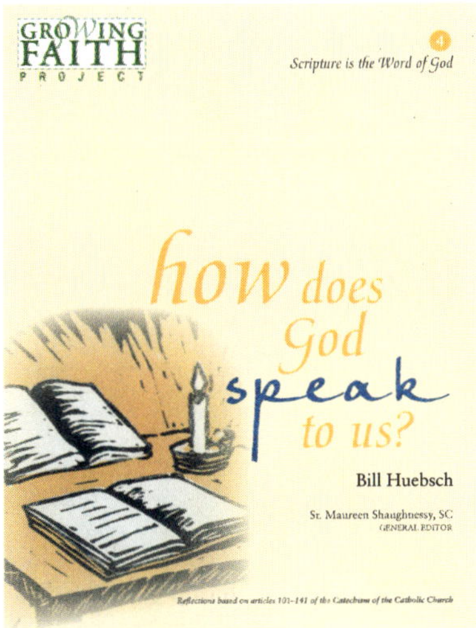

Excerpt from booklet #3

How we know

Christ, it seems,
deeply desired that all people
everywhere and throughout all time,
should have access to the Spirit of God,
which is the Spirit of Divine Love:
that wonderful divine power
which he himself knew so well.

For their part,
the apostles commissioned for this work
by Christ himself,
handed on what they had heard and seen.

This story did not end
when those who knew Christ personally died.
Bishops would follow bishops,
teaching as the apostles did.

The Church passes on to us all that she believes.

Engaging Scripture Effectively

Goal, Objectives, and Skill

The goal of *Engaging Scripture Effectively* is to help you make Scripture an integral part of your lives and also of those you teach.

Your objectives are

- to teach learners how to understand the Bible, according to their age level, as a *collection* of books, presenting it as a library;
- to learn methods for teaching about Sacred Scripture and using it in religion sessions;
- to help learners love and apply Scripture to their lives.

Skill

- Teach learners to make Scripture part of their lives, especially by living its teachings in your own life.

Preparation

- **Step One:** Experience the material in the *Spiritual Exercises*, and write your reflections.
- **Step Two:** Read booklets #3 *Why Do We Need the Church?* and #4 *How Does God Speak to Us?* of the *Growing Faith Project*, and do the reflections and exercises, recording your reflections.
- **Step Three:** Read the *Tools for Teaching* section carefully. Either at the group meeting or on your own, you will record your reflections and applications. If you are studying with a group, you will also share your experiences in teaching sessions.

Connecting Sessions

Consider how to best put into practice the skills you acquired in the last session as you study how to integrate Scripture more intentionally in your sessions.

Step One: Setting the Tone

This optional section offers examples of using Scripture in a religion session. Read and reflect on these sample activities. How do they help the children understand the Scripture passage better, according to their age level?

Sample Activities: Read to or tell your primary-age children the parable of the Good Shepherd from the Gospel of Luke, chapter 15, verses 1–7, using a children's Bible (you might show third graders how to find it). Ask the children what the shepherd in the story does. Why does he go after the sheep? How does that make the children feel? Let the children glue pieces of cotton onto drawings of sheep and have them write their names on their sheep to remind them of Jesus' love for them. With third graders you might have a "sheep search": hide figures of sheep around the room. Let the children pretend to be the shepherds and search for them.

> Catechesis must lead to "the gradual grasping of the whole truth about the divine plan" by introducing the disciples of Jesus to a knowledge of Tradition and of Scripture.
>
> GDC 85

Step Two: Importance of This Session

Part two is an introduction to teaching Scripture. Read this on your own. If you take part in the group sessions, share your reflections with your group.

How do you teach learners about the importance of Scripture in their lives?

- Teach them that the Bible is the written word of God and that we should listen with reverence.
- Show them how to read Scripture passages and how to integrate those passages in their daily lives.
- Teach about the Bible in your sessions with methods that are age-appropriate and engage your learners.

The revealed word of God is the heart and soul of faith formation. Keep a copy of the Bible on your prayer table or station and occasionally hold processions with the Bible to demonstrate reverence and honor for God's word. Using Scripture in your prayer experiences helps familiarize your learners with its words and fosters the practice of linking the Scriptures to their lives. Music is another excellent way to teach Scripture. Songs based on the psalms, the gospels, and other Scripture passages are available for every age. Beyond that, guide the learners in finding the messages and lessons God gives us in the Bible.

Integrating What You Have Just Learned

- ***Discuss with your group the importance of helping learners make Scripture an integral part of their lives. Reflect on your own experiences. Write down your thoughts and ideas.***

Notes

tips

- In addition to the Bible, keep a lectionary, a Sunday Missal, or another book with the Sunday readings according to the liturgical cycle on hand.
- Your own use of and attitude toward Scripture will be a model for the learners.

ON YOUR OWN

- *How often do you read and meditate on Scripture? Do you make it the guide of your life?*

Step Three: The Bible Is a Library

In order to show learners how to use the Bible, you can compare it to a library, something familiar to most learners. Read this on your own. If you take part in the group sessions, share your reflections with your group.

Refer to the section in the learners' text that talks about the Bible (for younger children this may be a very short piece).

The Bible is made up of seventy-three books. If you look at the contents page of your Bible, you will find that there are many different kinds of books.

- Some contain myths, legends, and parables meant to instruct.
- Others include biblical history and theology, poetry and romance.
- Still other books contain sagas or prayers or visions.

So we can consider the Bible to be a library with many different kinds of books—all inspired by God.

You can begin by showing the learners that the Bible is divided into the Old Testament and the New Testament. The Old Testament tells us how God created the world and gradually prepared a people for their salvation. The New Testament describes the life, miracles, and teachings of Jesus, as well as his passion and resurrection. It also relates the story and teachings of the early Church. Then, according to the learners' age level, when you use a passage from Scripture as part of the lesson or in an activity, or as part of your prayer, you can show them the section of the Bible it comes from.

tips

- Poetry in the psalms, history in Chronicles, wisdom writings in Proverbs, metaphorical writings in Genesis, narratives in the Gospels, pastoral writings in Pauline letters.

ON YOUR OWN

- *Choose your own favorite passages from the gospels. What do they tell you about who Jesus is for you at this moment?*

Integrating What You Have Just Learned

- ***Discuss with your group or reflect:** What means have you used to help the learners become more familiar with the Bible? What has worked and what hasn't? Explain. Write down your ideas, reflections, and suggestions.*

Notes

Step Four: Strategies for Teaching How to Use the Bible

From prayers to parables, the Bible offers a wealth of inspired reading for you and your learners. Read this on your own. If you take part in the group sessions, share your reflections with your group.

- Primary-age children are developing the skills that allow them to put pieces of knowledge together and to think in concrete concepts. Faith stories help shape their beliefs and values. Stress the teachings of the Old Testament stories and the parables of Jesus with hands-on activities—coloring pages, various kinds of puzzles, cutouts, etc. (whose degree of challenge depends on the age); music about the theme or the characters in the Scripture story; objects that relate to the story. Make a general timeline to show what place each of the major figures had in the history of the Bible. When you tell stories or read from the children's Bible, point out the general area the story is in.

- For intermediate-age children, story also plays an important role, and they want to know what is really true. They are very concerned about what is fair, and this influences their view of God. Stress the stories in the Bible, especially the parables of Jesus and the accounts of his miracles, that speak of God rewarding those who are faithful. Pray with psalms that refer to God as faithful, merciful, and just. Help them look up stories in the Scripture and act them out. Use Scripture-based word puzzles (crosswords, word searches) for introducing, reinforcing, or reviewing a theme.

- Middle-school learners are beginning to develop skills that allow them to think abstractly and reflect more deeply on faith stories and their meaning. Engage these learners in faith sharing based on the Sunday readings. Invite them to write or act out contemporary versions of some of the Scripture stories, especially the parables. Their longing for relationships is extended to God. Talk about relationships (not necessarily marriage relationships) in the Bible that led the persons closer to God (for example, Abraham and Sara; Moses and his wife Zipporah; David and Jonathan, his brother by adoption; Elizabeth and Zechariah; Mary and Joseph; Paul and the convert Lydia). Help them find where these examples are located in the Bible.

- Because the faith experience of youth and high school students is growing and their relationship with God is deepening, prayer and service to others becomes more meaningful. Help them find and read about persons of virtue from Scripture whom they can imitate in those areas. Especially focus on the life of Jesus and the call to discipleship. Encourage them to address the question of their vocation, to listen to the voice of the Spirit. Share with them gospel music and music based on the psalms that is relevant for their age.

- Make study of the Scriptures part of a comprehensive faith formation program for adults. Foster faith sharing on the parish's Question of the Week—based on the Sunday readings—in small groups, including parish ministry groups, small Christian communities, prayer groups, and so on. Both while studying and while reflecting on the readings, the adults will become more familiar with how to use the Bible.

Integrating What You Have Just Learned

- ***Share with your group what means each of you uses to teach your learners about Scripture. Or reflect on your own experiences. Which methods have been most effective? Write down the results of your discussions and reflections.***

Notes

ON YOUR OWN

- *Do you have a Bible in your home? Where do you keep it? When do you read the Scriptures with your family or household?*

Step Five: Methods for Teaching with the Scriptures

You have many methods at your disposal for using Scripture in your religion sessions. Read this on your own. If you take part in the group sessions, share your reflections with your group.

You can make the Scriptures an important part of your lessons in a variety of ways. These methods may be divided into four main groups: storytelling, activities, applying the message of God's word to daily life, and prayer experiences.

Stories and Activities

- Stories are popular with every age. First and second graders like to listen to the stories of the Bible; choose those they can best relate to. Involve the children in the telling of the story, for example, by having them repeat a name or phrase at specific points or by placing figures on a board as you tell it. Let the children retell the story in their own words, dress up and act it out, or do other activities such as drawing. These all allow you to evaluate their understanding and help them apply the message.

> Catechesis must be permeated with biblical and evangelical thought, spirit, and attitudes through constant use of and reference to the word of God.
>
> NDC 24C

- Third and fourth graders like to explore. They can work in groups and look up information on their own. Again involve the children in the storytelling in different ways, such as roleplaying or illustrating the story. Help them connect Scripture to life in concrete ways; for example, by acts of service such as making cards or small gifts for sick children.

- With fifth and sixth graders you will want to integrate their search for meaning, their growing awareness of right and wrong, and their sense of service to others. In teaching the Scriptures, stress the life and message of Jesus. Give them the opportunity to apply that message to moral situations. For example, invite them to roleplay a situation. Group work is also effective for this age. You might have the children form small groups and each make a chart of the major events in one of the gospels. Use hands-on activities to teach concepts, such as planting mustard seeds and decorating the pots. Engage their imagination. Let the learners take charge of their activities as much as possible. Encourage them to keep a journal to record their reflections on Scripture.

- Seventh and eighth graders, youth, and high school students can think abstractly and are more and more aware of the world outside their own. Peer pressure is a big concern. Offer them role models from Scripture. Use group discussion on the meaning of Scripture passages for their daily lives, even by presenting these passages in contemporary scriptural songs. Pose moral dilemmas they can solve by applying the gospel values. Use more involved hands-on activities, such as crafts and games, that draw on the learners' talents.

- For adults and in intergenerational gatherings, engage the participants in faith sharing based on the Sunday readings. Creatively engage adults and intergenerational groups with activities crafted around scriptural themes.

Prayer Experiences

- Music drawn from Scripture is especially effective with younger children. Strive to create a sense of wonder in their prayer experiences.
- With guidance, older learners are able to offer spontaneous and intercessory prayers based on the Scriptures. Help them relate the prayer experience to their lives. You can let them share in the planning of the prayer. You might have each of them write their own version of a psalm, for example.
- For all ages, develop prayer experiences centered on the Scriptures. Symbols used in connection with the Scripture passages add to the experience; for example, blessing with water for the story of Jesus and the disciples on the water, or a clay jar for the wedding at Cana. At each age level, engage all of the learners in some way in the prayer experience, whether as readers, as a chorus, as a leader, and so on. Rituals are especially meaningful.

As You End This Session

During this week take a few minutes each day, if possible, to become more familiar with the Bible.

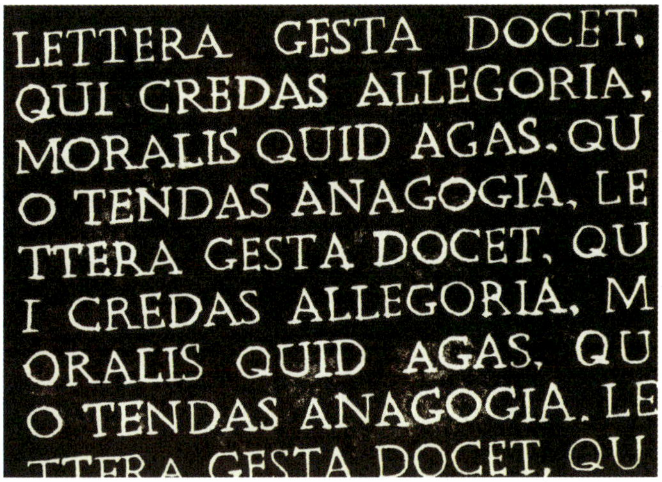

Integrating What You Have Just Learned

- ***Choose one age level and write out a brief outline for a lesson on Scripture. List the materials you will need.***
- ***If you are studying in a group, share and discuss your outline with the others. Record your reflections here.***

Notes

tips

- Various internet sites offer ideas for activities related to Scripture. Others will give you information and background. Do a search for your topic. For a list, see www.intothefields.org.
- Use maps to show where different events in the Bible took place, or the travels of figures in the Bible.

ON YOUR OWN

- *How do you use Scripture in your own prayer?*

Walking in God's Presence

You Are Near

■ ***Begin by closing your eyes and breathing deeply for a few moments as a way of centering yourself. When you feel ready, listen to the song "You Are Near" (track 7 on the CD), allowing a few moments for silence at the end.***

■ ***Here are the lyrics to the song:***

Yahweh, I know you are near,
standing always at my side.
You guard me from the foe,
and you lead me in ways everlasting.

Lord, you have searched my heart,
and you know when I sit and when I stand.
Your hand is upon me protecting me from
death, keeping me from harm.

Where can I run from your love?
If I climb to the heavens you are there;
if I fly to the sunrise or sail beyond the sea,
still I'd find you there.

Marvelous to me are your works!
How profound are your thoughts, my Lord!
Even if I could count them
they number as the stars
you would still be there.

Song Notes

Now listen to the song again, but this time pay special attention to any words, images, or feelings it calls forth in you. If there are any words or images that make you uncomfortable, note those as well. Write these down so you can recall them later.

Notes

■ *When you're ready, continue by prayerfully reading the following reflection.*

A Time for Prayer and a Time for Labor

One of the great paradoxes in the history of Christian spirituality is found in the dichotomy set up between the sphere of one's prayer (contemplation), and one's action (the place where we work and play). The great dilemma for many spiritual writers, from St. Thomas Aquinas to Thomas Merton, has been to discover a balance between the two realms. How can I be a spiritual person while living in a secular world?

For anyone intent on growing in their relationship with God and deepening their faith, time for private prayer is an essential element. But the practical struggle for many comes down to these questions: When during my busy life can I fit in time for prayer? How much time do I need? How can I deal with all the distractions that pull me away from this contemplative time of my day?

These are real and serious questions. For many spiritual writers, the time of prayer and contemplation is seen as the higher calling and a more perfect way to live one's life. St. Thomas Aquinas and St. Augustine, even though they lamented the "sterility" of the contemplative life, still admitted that it was a superior way of living to that of teaching and preaching.

How can serving others be a form of prayer?

Spend a few moments to reflect on your own life. Ask yourself: How does time for prayer fit into my day? Is it a struggle? Do I have a prayer routine that helps give structure to my life? How do I balance prayer with all the other things that demand my time and attention? Write your answers here.

Notes

■ ***When you finish, continue with the reflection.***

Contemplation in Action

St. Ignatius of Loyola offers another perspective that might assist us in finding the balance between these seemingly polar elements of our lives. Ignatius' desire was that his followers should live and work in the heart of the world, in the very midst of people going about their lives. He did not envision his society to be like the contemplative orders of his time where individuals withdrew from the world, freeing themselves from everyday distractions in the pursuit of prayer and spiritual things.

The Ignatian vision is for a person to become a "contemplative in action." By this term, he didn't just mean that at one moment we pray, and the next moment we enter into the activity of our life, balancing the two and moving back and forth between them. Rather, for Ignatius the activity of our life becomes the foundation for our prayer, the place where we see the hand of God at work and are moved to prayer in the very midst of our activity. Our prayer flows from and through and back to the activities of our daily life.

What rituals
do you use that allow
God to fill your life?

Contemplation is not just an ascetical exercise, but an affective one. It moves one's very heart and mind toward God. Our goal is to grow in a kind of spirituality where God becomes part of the very fabric of our daily lives, not compartmentalized to the times of private prayer and public worship. We strive to develop an attention to God's presence throughout our day and experience moments of contemplation right in the midst of our activity.

Let me provide an image of this. When we deeply love someone, we go about our daily activities carrying thoughts, memories, and feelings of our beloved in our hearts. Although the other person is not physically present, he or she is in our soul. Our minds flow back to the beloved when it has a free moment or when something reminds us of him or her. This is what Ignatius envisions for a person in love with God. We carry God with us as we go through our day, even when we are not formally at prayer.

Take a moment now to reflect on the following questions. How might I bring God into the routine of my day? What might I do that would help me be more aware of God as I go about my activities? How might I develop the habit of appropriating moments with God during my day? Write down your thoughts.

Notes

When you're ready, continue with the reflection.

Carry God With You

Prayer is a relationship of our whole being, mind, and heart, with the God who loves us. Just as we surround our human relationships with symbols and rituals that assist us in keeping them alive and healthy, should we not look for ways to do the same to deepen our relationship with God? At our workplace we might keep a photograph of our spouse and children on our desk as a way of keeping them present to us. We might regularly call home at lunchtime to check in and see how things are going. At bedtime we might kiss our children goodnight and say "I love you." In time, our relationship grows deeper through the attentiveness these habits and rituals enable us to give to the ones we love.

The habit of making God part of the fabric of our lives can be aided significantly by similar symbols and rituals. As we endeavor to become contemplatives in action, we need symbols to remind us. Some carry a rosary or a Sacred Heart medal. Others make sure that there is a crucifix on their wall or a Bible on the nightstand. These kinds of religious symbols become anchor points in our consciousness.

We can also take advantage of the daily rituals of our lives to help us. Things like getting out of bed in the morning, driving to work, sitting down to eat, walking the dog, and doing the dishes can become ritual opportunities to allow God to permeate our consciousness.

The Time of Prayer

■ *For a few minutes close your eyes and imagine God's face before you. Rest in the loving gaze of your God. This is the God who loves you so much more than you know, and who wants to be more a part of your life.*

■ *When you're ready, end with the following prayer, or better, with a prayer in your own words.*

■ *If you'd like to make notes to help you recall your time of prayer, you may do that it the space provided.*

God of my heart,
you know me better than I know myself
and you understand that my heart really wants you
to be more a part of my life.
Teach me, Lord, as you would patiently teach a child,
how to allow you to permeate my daily activities.
I don't think I yet understand
how much you love me and want to have me close.
Thank you, Lord, from the depths of my heart,
for your steadfast, enduring love.

When you are ready, end your time by praying the Our Father.

The Growing Faith Project booklets for this session are #7 and #34.

7 God is One in Three

Content summary of booklet #7

- *We believe in one God.*
- *God alone is the origin of life and our ultimate goal.*
- *God remains a mystery beyond words.*
- *The mystery of the Trinity is the central Christian mystery. God is three in one: Father, Son, and Holy Spirit.*

This booklet makes reference to articles 232–267 in the *Catechism of the Catholic Church.*

34 Society and human dignity

Content summary of booklet #34

- *There is a likeness between the unity of the Trinity and the community that we ought to establish among ourselves.*
- *Society ought to promote the exercise of virtue, not obstruct it. Society should be organized around a sense of value and the common good of all.*
- *Public authority is exercised legitimately only if it is committed to the common good of society. To attain this it must employ morally acceptable means.*
- *The equal dignity of persons requires the effort to reduce excessive social and economic inequalities.*

This booklet makes reference to articles 1877–1948 in the *Catechism of the Catholic Church.*

Excerpt from booklet #7

The Basis of Our Faith

This is a story about love,
tremendous,
powerful,
life-changing love.
At baptism, a Christian is signed
in the name of the Father,
and of the Son,
and of the Holy Spirit.
Love.
The cross of Christ is traced on our bodies
as we profess this faith
and all we believe rests on this.
Love.

That cross, and our belief in God,
results only from God's love for us.
We give a name to this wonderful and mysterious belief:
we call it the Most Holy Trinity.

The Trinity is the central mystery of Christian faith and life.

Building a Community of Love

Goal, Objectives, and Skill

The goal of *Building a Community of Love* is to facilitate the building of an appropriate community of love among your learners by instilling a sense of respect, order, affirmation, and love for one another.

Your objectives are

- to formulate the rules of good conduct for your religion sessions, with the help of your learners, if possible;
- to learn about the different factors that might motivate a child to misbehave, and to treat these behavioral issues as Jesus would;
- to learn ways to foster understanding, respect, communication, and collaboration among your learners.

Skill

- Build a community of love among your learners, modeled after the communion of love of the Trinity and the example of Jesus.

Preparation

- **Step One:** Engage the material in the *Spiritual Exercises*, and write your reflections about your experience.
- **Step Two:** Read booklet #7 *What Is the Love of the Trinity?* and booklet #34 *How Should We Live as a Community?* of the *Growing Faith Project*, and do the reflections and exercises, recording your reflections.
- **Step Three:** Read the *Tools for Teaching* section carefully. It is important to articulate your reflections and applications in writing or verbally, whether alone or working as part of a group. If you are studying with a group, take advantage of the opportunity to share your experiences in learning sessions.

Connecting Sessions

In the previous three sessions you have studied some of the principles of human development and learning, as well as steps to take to make liturgy and Scripture an important part of your teaching. In this session you will learn how to build a community of love among your learners, so your sessions will be positive experiences for them.

Step One: Setting the Tone

This optional section introduces you to the importance of communication and collaboration in building community. Read and reflect on the sample exercise.

Sample Exercise: The participants form three groups. Each group is given a box of materials (cloth, different objects, and some paper and pencils). The members of each group will choose a parable to act out, using the materials in the box. However, they won't be allowed to use dialogue in their presentation. Each group, in turn, makes their presentation and the members of the other groups are to guess what parable is being enacted.

> Catechesis prepares the Christian to live in community and to participate actively in the life and mission of the Church.
>
> GDC 20.5

Step Two: Importance of This Session

The comparison of changing "water" into "wine" introduces you to means for achieving positive discipline in your sessions. Read this on your own. If you take part in the group sessions, share your reflections with your group.

How to facilitate the learners in building a community of love:

- Formulate the rules of good conduct for your religion sessions.
- Learn about the different factors that might motivate a child to misbehave and treat each behavioral issue as Jesus would, giving your learners the example of how to treat one another.
- Foster understanding, respect, communication, and collaboration among your learners.

A wise educator, Sr. Maxine Inkel, was once meditating on the gospel story of the wedding at Cana. She had been thinking for days about how to present the joy of teaching to other catechists and teachers. "It's just a matter of learning from Jesus how to turn the water of potentially negative situations into the wine of joy. Turning water into wine can become a wonderful lifelong habit," she later wrote.[1]

In this session we will study how we can take the "water" of a child with an attitude, find out what is behind it, and turn it into the "wine" of a child's newfound sense of worth.

Jesus himself said, "I am the vine, you are the branches. Those who abide in me and I in them bear much fruit, because apart from me you can do nothing" (John 15:5). When we bring the wine of love into our religion sessions, the love of the Trinity, the love of Jesus, and our own love for our learners, the Holy Spirit will touch their hearts through us and help form a community of love.

Integrating What You Have Just Learned

- ***Discuss with the group and reflect on the words of Sr. Maxine. How have you tried to build an atmosphere of respect and love among the learners? Write down your reflections.***

Notes

[1] *What Would Jesus Do? A Catechist's Guide to Discipline,* Twenty-Third Publications.

ON YOUR OWN

- *What do the words understanding, respect, communication, and collaboration mean to you?*

Step Three: Preparing the Soil

This section describes some preparatory steps for establishing positive discipline in the learning session. Read this on your own. If you take part in the group sessions, share your reflections with your group.

Continuing the metaphor of the good wine, if you want to build communities of love in your religion sessions you need to "prepare the soil" in three ways:

- be prepared, confident of your calling, and desirous of helping your learners encounter Christ (Session 1 of *Tools for Teaching*);
- make your teaching area a sacred space where learners feel comfortable and welcome (Session 2);
- prepare appealing lessons that immerse the learners in a true learning experience that leads them to commitment to Christ (Session 3).

The process of conversion is lifelong, so building a community of love is an ongoing process. Discipleship is a commitment to ongoing growth and development.

ON YOUR OWN

Do you tend to focus on the "water" rather than the "wine" in your religion sessions? In what ways can you improve?

Another way of preparing the soil is to set realistic rules about behavior during your sessions. If you don't clearly set limits for your learners, they will try to define them by trial and error. You will want to give the reasons for the rules, stressing especially that you want them all to respect one another and feel safe and secure during your sessions.

Make the rules as simple and as few as possible, and state them in a positive way. For example, instead of saying, "Do not talk while another person is talking," say, "Listen to one another with respect." Whenever possible, involve your learners in establishing the rules and also in deciding on the consequences of not keeping them as well as the reward for keeping them. By doing this you transfer ownership of their behavior to them. You might ask them to sign a covenant in which they agree to observe the rules, and, when appropriate, send home a copy to each of their families.

Integrating What You Have Just Learned

On your own or with your study group, formulate a list of rules that you think are important for fostering a climate of respect, learning, and understanding among the learners. Then reduce that list to the five rules you consider the most important. Write your reflections and ideas about rules here.

Notes

Step Four: Cultivating the Vines

Sometimes children with behavior issues have other underlying problems. Read this on your own. If you take part in the group sessions, share your reflections with your group.

Most are familiar with the child or youth who is distracted or distracting, one who has an attitude, another who seems totally bored, yet another who likes to be the "class clown," and one who likes to "push your buttons." Sometimes, our best efforts to modify such behavior don't seem to bear much fruit.

This may well be an opportunity to get to know the learners better. Often, disruptive behavior has roots beyond what we can immediately perceive. For example, a learner may be looking for the attention he or she does not receive at home, or may actually be hurting inside because of a situation at home, and does not know how to express it. He or she may have a poor self-image and is afraid of being laughed at.

What are some steps you can take to discover whether a learner's behavior is a symptom of some other problem? First of all, of course, pray for those learners who "act out" in your group. Pray for the gifts of the Spirit to address the situation with compassion and love. Following that, you can try some of these other approaches. Keep in mind to always respect the privacy of the learner. When meeting with a learner, make sure another adult is present or visible.

- Talk with the learner privately, making the meeting as informal as possible so the learner will feel more relaxed. You might start with some words of affirmation, then ask if there is some problem outside of the religion sessions. The learners themselves may not always know what the problem is—but this is a start. You may even note something in their body language or their eyes that hint at feelings below the surface.
- Carefully study the learner's responses in the group—both written and oral. These often furnish clues as to state of mind and feelings.
- Engage the learner in an activity in which he or she plays an important part. The way the learner relates to the others and the reactions you observe may indicate where there is a problem.
- The lighting or ventilation in the room may be poor, or the learners may be fatigued. The latter problem can be at least partially addressed by giving a brief "time out" for a break. Overactive learners, on the other hand, may require more involvement in activities.
- Discuss what you observe in your religion sessions with your learner's family and ask for their suggestions.

Whatever your manner of engaging this challenge, let it be based on knowledge of and love for the learners as unique persons, for whom you are called to be not only leader but, in imitation of Jesus, comforter, companion, healer, someone who empowers and encourages them in their journey.

Integrating What You Have Just Learned

- ***Without referring to names or grades, discuss or reflect on experiences you have had with behavior problems. How did you address these problems? What worked and what did not work? Write your reflections and ideas.***

Notes

tips

- To avoid confusion and even chaos when assigning an activity, give clear directions and repeat them more than once.

ON YOUR OWN

- *Do you respect each and every learner you teach? Do you make the effort to treat all your learners with equal love and compassion?*

Step Five: Gathering the Grapes

This section describes four qualities needed for building a community of love. Read this alone. If you take part in the group sessions, share your reflections with the group.

A man who took great pride in his lawn once found himself with a large crop of dandelions. He tried every method he knew to get rid of them. Still they plagued him. Finally he wrote to the Department of Agriculture. He enumerated all the things he had tried and closed his letter with the question: "What shall I do now?"

In due course the reply came: "We suggest you learn to love them."

In your religion sessions, teach and foster certain qualities in your learners that will allow learning to flourish more easily because a community of love is established. The community won't be perfect, but it will be in process. The qualities are understanding, respect, communication, and collaboration.

- *Understanding* is the first step or building block. When learners are taught to understand one another and to appreciate each other's differences as gifts, they are less inclined to hurt others or to have problems in relationships. They become less self-centered and their perspective is widened.

How do you foster a community of love among your learners?

- *Respect* is based on understanding. As learners expect to receive respect, so must they be willing to freely give it. Young learners especially, that is, children and teens, often are not shown this respect in other areas of their lives. Respect helps build up their self-image and esteem and makes them realize their worth as children of God.

- As respect grows, so does the desire and even the need to *communicate*, especially for young adolescents, youth, and high school students, for whom relationships are becoming more and more important. Encourage them to express themselves freely but also with respect for the feelings and viewpoints of others.

- *Collaboration* is an important skill for building a community of love. Learning how to work together is essential if the learners are to fulfill their calling as disciples of Jesus to carry on his mission.

Do your best to foster the above and other qualities in your learners and offer the example of Jesus, and you and your learners will be united with the true vine of the Master.

Strategies for Fostering a Community of Love

Help learners develop a community of love by using these and similar methods.

- Discuss the learners' experience of the diversity of people coming together to celebrate Eucharist, which can be a model for them. In the Sunday Assembly they see the collaboration necessary for a celebration that is reverent and that promotes the "full, conscious, and active" participation of those present: the collaboration of the pastor or presider, the lectors, the ministers of the Eucharist, the altar servers, the music ministers, the ministers of hospitality, and finally the members of the Assembly itself. Such collaboration requires respect and understanding as well as good communication within each group and among the groups.

- Find and share with your learners (or have them look up) passages in the gospels in which Jesus taught or demonstrated each of the qualities of a community of love. You will also find such passages in St. Paul,'s and in other New Testament writings. You can make these passages the basis for faith sharing, a prayer experience, role-playing, music, or activities. Examples of such passages are found in Matthew 10:40–42 (understanding, respect); 10:1–14 (communication and collaboration); 5:43–48 (respect, love); Luke 5:17–26 (respect); 6:27–36 (respect, understanding, love); 6:37–42 (understanding, respect); 9:10–17 (collaboration); 15:11–32 (respect, understanding, collaboration); John 4:1–15 (respect, understanding, communication); 8:1–11 (respect, understanding, communication).

- Role-play with the older learners. Have them act out what they would do in different situations requiring one or more of the four qualities. For example, what would they do if a new person joined their class; if they met someone of a different cultural or ethnic background; if they wanted to express a different opinion on some issue; if someone tried to start an argument with them; if they had to work with someone they didn't like; if someone took something that belonged to them; and so on.

- Involve your learners in group work, according to their age level, that requires communication and collaboration to accomplish a task, for example, the preparation of a prayer service, or, for young learners, a certain type of game or other activity.

- Invite learners—again according to age level—to plan together and carry out some form of service or outreach activity.

- As noted above, involve your learners in formulating and enforcing the basic rules of behavior, as well as the rewards or punishments.

As You End This Session

Be aware this week of opportunities to build a community of love—at home, at work, with friends.

Integrating What You Have Just Learned

- ***Discuss with the group and reflect: How does each of the above strategies foster the exercise of understanding, respect, communication, and collaboration? Write your reflections and ideas below.***

Notes

tips

- Reinforce good behavior with positive affirmation. But don't overdo it.
- When a situation arises—whether you've run out of material, or are facing a behavior problem, or are pressed for time—remain calm and in control.

ON YOUR OWN

- *How do you exemplify the above qualities for your learners? What are your strengths? Where can you improve?*

Prepare the Way

Come, Lord Jesus

■ *Following the pattern of past exercises, find a quiet place and spend a few moments centering yourself. Close your eyes and take several slow, deep breaths. Imagine that you are breathing in the Spirit of God. When you feel prepared, listen to the song "Come, Lord Jesus" (track 8 on the CD). Keep your eyes closed and simply let yourself experience the music and let the words seep into your soul. Spend a few moments of quiet at the end.*

■ *Then, when you feel ready, listen to the song again. But this time follow along with the lyrics. Pay special attention to any words, images, or feelings that seem to resonate in your heart.*

■ *Here are the song lyrics:*

Come, Lord Jesus. Come and visit
your people.
We await your coming. Come, O Lord.

And on that day a branch shall spring
from Jesse's tree.
A sign of hope that life is born
to those who wait.

And on that day a hope shall rise
for all who seek.
A light will shine for those
who walk amid the gloom.

And on that day the lame shall dance
and leap for joy.
The deaf shall hear,
the blind shall see the face of God.

■ *When you have finished, spend a few minutes writing what seemed to be important in your listening.*

Song Notes

■ ***Continue by slowly reading through the following reflection.***

We Await Your Coming

We are Advent people. We spend so much of our time in a waiting mode. Think of how many hours, days, weeks, and years you spend caught in traffic, standing in lines, looking forward to the birth of a child, or sitting beside the bed of a sick loved one. And in the final years of life, we wait for death to visit us.

The important question is not that we wait, but how we go about it. Some of us are more patient than others, not needing to control the timing and outcomes of life, but we've all experienced moments of great frustration and disappointment. We often wait with great hope and anticipation, but we can also get anxious, angry, cynical, and sometimes, downright ugly when things don't move as quickly as we'd hoped. You would think, with all the practice we have, we would grow more graceful in our waiting!

Beyond these human experiences, as people of Christian faith, we wait in hope for something bigger than ourselves. Like the Hebrew people of the Old Testament, we're waiting for the promise of our God to be fulfilled. We've heard the promise of God's kingdom of peace, justice, and equality voiced in the Scripture texts on Sunday morning. And we've known similar dreams for humanity deep in our souls. We long for the day when sin and death are no more.

What do you dream and hope that Christ will accomplish in you?

The challenge of our waiting is not to become cynical, or, in the end, to despair. There are many voices that tell us we're foolish for believing that things will someday be different. Our own frustrating, disappointing experiences seem to mock our faith in God's word. We complain, and grumble, and flirt with giving up this way of faith. Yet in the end God helps us to hold on. The promise of God's kingdom stands clear and bold in the midst of our despair and cynicism.

Spend a few moments reflecting on how you go about waiting. Ask yourself: Do I wait in faith? Have I become cynical? Do I really trust the promise of God? Write your answers below.

Notes

■ ***Now continue with the reflection.***

It's important for us to remember that Jesus of Nazareth was a Jewish man. The Old Testament is his family history, the story of his ancestors. There is no real way to understand Jesus without understanding the context in which he lived. As a child and young man he learned from his parents of the great promise God had made to Abraham so many generations ago.

> *Now the Lord said to Abram, "Go from your country and your kindred and your father's house to the land that I will show you. I will make of you a great nation, and I will bless you, and make your name great, so that you will be a blessing. I will bless those who bless you, and the one who curses you I will curse; and in you all the families of the earth shall be blessed" (Genesis 12:1–3).*

This was Jesus' spiritual background. Along with many generations of the Hebrew people, he lived his life holding on to the promise of God, waiting in hope for the fulfillment of God's word. He read the Hebrew Scripture stories that tell over and over of God's unfailing faithfulness to Israel. God brought them from slavery, safely through the sea, across the barren desert, and finally to the Promised Land. God comforted them in sorrow, encouraged them in disappointment, admonished their stubbornness, and forgave their unfaithfulness over and over again. There is no obstacle to God's word. And finally, God promised them a Savior.

Take a moment here to ask yourself: Is God's promise alive in my soul? Have I grown cynical and skeptical? Remember back to the second exercise and the litany you wrote of God's faithfulness. Write a few sentences of your thoughts.

Notes

■ ***When you're ready, continue with the reflection.***

Herald of Glad Tidings

But Zion said, "The Lord has forsaken me,
my Lord has forgotten me."
Can a woman forget her nursing-child,
or show no compassion for the
child of her womb?
Even these may forget,
yet I will not forget you.
See, I have inscribed you on
the palms of my hands;
your walls are continually before me.
(Isaiah 49:14–16)

How then, as teachers and catechists, can we help people on their journey of faith during this time between God's promise and the coming of the kingdom? Perhaps we can look to John the Baptist, one of the main characters of the Advent season, for a model. The Baptist makes it very clear that he is not the Messiah, the Promised One. He is just the herald of the glad tidings, the one announcing the coming of Christ. As teachers, then, we must be careful that the spotlight is not on us, but on the One who comes after us, the one whose sandals we are not worthy to carry (Matthew 3:11). We are not the Good News; Jesus is. We must take care that our egos don't get in the way of the real message. Like John the Baptist, we strive to keep our eyes on Jesus. We are like a prism that manifests the beauty of God's light to other hearts. But we ourselves are not the light, just small pieces of polished glass.

So too, like John, we might not see the fruit of our labors. The work of the Spirit in a person's soul takes time. It is God's work, not ours to claim. Our role is that of preparing the fertile soil in which the seed of God's word is planted, where it can flourish and grow. We are like the farmer that tills the earth, plants the seed, and then waits. It is God who sends the rain and the sun that bring the seed to fruitfulness. We must wait with patience.

You prepare the soil where God's word can flourish.

This might be an opportunity for you to take an inventory of your own teaching, your motivations and zeal. Ask yourself: Is my goal to introduce people to the person of Jesus or merely to articles of doctrine? Do I believe what I teach? Do I feel passion for the Good News of Jesus and teach with firm conviction? Write a few of your reflections below.

Notes

The Time of Prayer

■ *As in previous exercises, we now end our time of reflection with a "colloquy," a heartfelt prayer in our own words, in the presence of God. We are friends talking to a friend. Begin with the words provided below, and then continue as your heart moves you. Ask God for what you desire.*

■ *If you would like to make notes to help you recall your time of prayer, you may do that it the space provided.*

God of steadfast love,
you always keep your promises.
Teach me how to prepare the way for your coming
into the hearts of those you entrust to my care.
Give me the right words,
and let me not get in the way of your work in them.
You have sent your Son, Jesus, to show us the way to your kingdom.
With all of creation I wait in hope
for the day of his coming in glory.
And, dear Lord, teach me patience as I wait.

When you are ready, end by praying the Our Father.

The Growing Faith Project booklets for this session are #8 and #9.

8 God, the Creator

Content summary of booklet #8

- *In the creation of the world and of us, God gave the first and universal witness to almighty love and wisdom.*
- *God alone created the universe freely, directly, and without any help.*
- *God created the universe and keeps it in existence through Jesus Christ, in whom all things continue in being, and by the Spirit, the giver of life.*
- *The existence of physical and moral evil is a mystery.*

This booklet makes reference to articles 268–324 in the *Catechism of the Catholic Church*.

9 God creates everything

Content summary of booklet #9

- *Angels are God's messengers and our protectors.*
- *God willed the diversity of creatures and their own particular goodness, interdependence, and order.*
- *God destined all material creatures for the good of the human race.*
- *We humans are a unity of body and soul.*

This booklet makes reference to articles 325–373 in the *Catechism of the Catholic Church*.

Excerpt from booklet #8

The Creator

The Book of Genesis,
the first book of the entire Bible,
begins with these words:
"In the beginning...
God created the heavens and the earth."
We also begin with this:
Divine Love provides us
with the generous and free gift of creation.
Divine Love is eternal,
but creation and the world are not.

They occur within history,
within time,
with a beginning and an end.
And they are part of how Divine Love
"shares love with others," we might say.

God alone made heaven and earth.

Teaching Others as God Teaches Us

Goal, Objectives, and Skill

The goal of *Teaching Others as God Teaches Us* is to explore what is called the "Divine pedagogy," that is, to explore how God is revealed to us and how we can use this process as a model for our catechesis.

Your objectives are

- to understand the characteristics of God's self-revelation as the source and model for catechesis;
- to relate these characteristics to catechesis;
- to learn strategies to help learners recognize God's voice in their lives.

Skill

- Listen to and learn from God's self-revelation in order to model our teaching on it.

Preparation

- **Step One:** Engage the material in the *Spiritual Exercises*, and write your reflections.
- **Step Two:** Read booklets #8 *How Did God Create the World?* and #9 *How Are We in God's Image?* of the *Growing Faith Project*, and do the reflections and exercises, recording your reflections.
- **Step Three:** Read the *Tools for Teaching* section carefully. It is important to articulate your reflections and applications in writing or verbally, whether alone or working as part of a group. If you are studying with a group, take advantage of the opportunity to share your experiences in learning sessions.

Connecting Sessions

After studying ways to build a community of love in the last session, you will now focus on listening to and learning from God's self-revelation as a model for teaching.

Step One: Setting the Tone

This optional section is to introduce you to the topic of teaching learners as God teaches us.

One summer two friends were doing missionary work in the hills of Appalachia. They were deeply impressed by the faith of the people they met during their visits. Amid the poverty and hardships the people faced, their main comfort was their belief in God's presence and care for them.

One of the friends remembers one elderly man in particular. He lived in a broken-down trailer with very little furniture and no electricity. When the missionaries offered him a copy of the Bible, he suddenly raised his hand to his lips. "Listen!" They followed his gaze to the tall pines that were swaying in the wind.

"When I feel lonely or blue, I listen to God's voice speaking to me—in the trees, in the sky. I know he cares about me. That's what matters."

Step Two: Importance of This Session

This session focuses on ways in which we can model our teaching on the teaching of God and Jesus. Read this on your own. If you take part in the group sessions, share your reflections with your group.

How do you model God's way of revelation in your teaching and catechesis?

- Understand the characteristics of God's self-revelation as the source and model for catechesis.
- Apply these characteristics to catechesis.
- Use strategies to help learners recognize God's voice in their lives.

Gestures, signs, and objects in teaching, rituals and silence in prayer, can be means for teaching as God teaches us. Helping learners see God's hand and hear God's voice in the events of the day is another means. Jesus' love for the poor and the outcast of society is also an example for us to follow in our teaching.

God's pedagogy
is the source and model
of the pedagogy
of the faith.
NDC 28

Integrating What You Have Just Learned

- ***Discuss with your group or reflect on the importance of helping learners recognize God in their daily lives. What are some other means for doing this besides those mentioned? Write your reflections and ideas.***

Notes

tips

- Keep a box with different objects in it that you can use as part of your lessons. They don't need to be only religious items; for example, a pretty stone, a small box, a piece of fabric, a toy or two, may all come in handy to impart a message.

ON YOUR OWN

- *Choose a favorite gospel passage. Does Jesus use any means besides words to convey his message? If so, do they make the message more striking or memorable for you?*

Step Three: God's Revelation as Our Model

How can God's revelation be a model for our catechesis? Read this on your own. If you take part in the group sessions, share your reflections with your group.

God's loving revelation of the communion of Father, Son, and Holy Spirit is a model for all catechetical ministry. We find the fullness of God's self-revelation is found in Jesus, the Word made flesh.

Reflect on some of the characteristic elements of God's self-communication to us.

- God bestowed revelation on generation after generation, adapting the message to different people; God made a covenant, an everlasting pledge of love.
- God transformed events in the life of the people into divine encounters.
- Jesus is both truly human and truly God.
- Christ's relationship with his disciples offers the model for catechetical methods. He engaged them in conversation. He taught them to pray.
- Jesus used words, signs, wonders, silence, and gestures; he showed affection for the poor, sinners, and marginalized.
- Christ invited his listeners to a whole new manner of life, built on faith, hope, and love.
- The Holy Spirit unfolds God's plan of salvation through the Church.

God's word is powerful and brings about the effect it intends. "More than a message, it is an event that inspires, even compels, action" (NDC #27). Through the grace of the Spirit, God brings about conversion to Christ and our profession of belief.

Catechesis must present God's revelation to the people of today in the languages, signs, and cultural expressions that they can understand. It addresses all the aspects of our faith: knowledge, liturgy, Christian life, and prayer.

Integrating What You Have Just Learned

- ***Discuss with your group members or reflect on your own on any three characteristics of God's revelation. What do these mean to you as a catechist? Write the results of your reflections.***

Notes

ON YOUR OWN

- *What does the example of God's self-communication mean to you personally, in your own ministry as catechist? Which elements mean the most to you? Why?*

Step Four: God's Self-Revelation and Catechesis

Catechesis takes its inspiration from the elements of God's communication to us. Read this on your own. If you take part in the group sessions, share your reflections with your group.

Because catechesis is the proclamation of God's revelation, it draws its inspiration from what the NDC calls "the pedagogy of God" (28B). The relationship between them can be spelled out in the following ways.

- Talk about God's great love for us, experienced especially in the plan of salvation in the person of Jesus Christ. You can show your learners how much God loves them by inviting them to think about the wonders in their lives, and helping them see God acting in the events, great and small, of everyday. You can especially use activities, prayers, and other means that point to Jesus as the greatest Gift of God's love.
- Emphasize that God took the initiative in calling us to a personal relationship, yet God respects our freedom in responding to this call. Examples of this calling can be found in Scripture and in the lives of the saints and contemporary Christian witnesses. Point out the difference their choices made in salvation history and in our present society.
- Discuss or illustrate the dignity of the human person, made in the image of God and called to a unique relationship with God. Growing in that relationship requires continual conversion. Ask in what ways we are different from other creatures God has placed on this earth. Use activities that highlight the dignity of the human person and our place in the world, including stewardship.
- Emphasize that Jesus is the center of our lives and of God's plan for our salvation. Our Christian vocation is to encounter and follow Jesus. Experiencing the mystery of Jesus, especially as found in the gospels, permeates your teaching, celebrations, and way of living.
- Our call to relationship with God is a model for our call to relationship with our brothers and sisters. Prayer, outreach, acts of justice, the effort to build a community of love are all ways you can use to teach how to grow in this relationship.
- Help your learners experience the joy of belonging to your community of faith.
- Use signs and symbols in your teaching, to link words and actions, teaching and experience.
- Rely on the inspiration of the Holy Spirit and teach your learners how the Holy Spirit is present and active in the Church. Encourage them, through activities, prayer, and action, to point out the Spirit's presence in persons, in the liturgy, in the teaching of the Church, and so on.

Integrating What You Have Just Learned

- ***What do accounts of creation in Genesis (1:1—2:4 and 2:4b–25) tell us about our belief in God, in the act of creation, in the goodness of creation, of the dignity of the human person? Write your reflections and ideas.***

Notes

tips

- Depending on where you meet, make sure you have at least one or two religious images (pictures, statues, icons) visible for every session, as a visual reminder for your learners.

ON YOUR OWN

- *Is teaching about God's love, Jesus' love, central to your catechesis? How?*

Step Five: Hearing and Listening to God's Voice

In addition to Revelation, God teaches us through creation and liturgy. Read this on your own. If you take part in the group sessions, share your reflections with your group.

St. Augustine wrote a beautiful reflection on finding God in creation. "Heaven and earth and everything within them call to me to love you.... What is the object of my love? I asked the earth and it replied, 'Not I.' I asked everything in the world, and they said the same thing. I asked the oceans, the creeping creatures, and they replied, 'We are not your God; look further.' I asked the wind and the air and they said, 'I am not God.' I asked the sun, the moon, and the stars, and they replied, 'We are not the God you are looking for.' I said to all of them, 'If you are not God, tell me something about him.' And they cried out with one voice: 'He made us.' My question was in my gazing on them, and their reply was in their beauty."[1]

> God first revealed himself through creation and continually provides evidence of himself in the created order.
>
> NDC 16A

[1] St. Augustine, *Confessions*, Book X, #8–9.

These words of St. Augustine bring us back to the accounts of creation. In the accounts in Genesis (1:1—2:4 and 2:4b–25) besides words God uses gestures and signs: "God separated the light from the darkness"; "God blessed [the man and woman]"; "the Lord God formed man from the dust of the ground." The account would not be as meaningful or as vivid without them. What meaning do those gestures and signs have? What are the signs of God's revelation, of God's voice, in creation today?

Help your learners listen to God's voice in the events of our time and of their own lives. The needs of a friend or a family member, the joy of friendship or the sorrow of a loss, the desire to serve, a tragic disaster, the use or abuse of animals and of natural resources, immigration, prejudice, the cry of the poor and the oppressed—in all these and more they can hear God's voice.

Most times God's voice is drowned out by the noise of the modern world, by the proliferation of media, by advertising, by the voices of power, by our own inattentiveness. So how do you learn to listen?

Silence is an important means, silence not just in the space around you, but silence of the mind and heart. Prayer, too, is essential. Silence and prayer enable you to discern, to discover and respond to God's voice.

Another place where you hear God's voice is in your experience of the liturgy. God is revealed in so many ways (word, sacrament, assembly, presider, ritual). That is why the liturgy provides moments of silence, so you can reflect on the experience. You can perceive God's presence and action in the words and actions, the signs and rituals of the liturgy, as well as how they impact your lives. You are then able to carry your experience of the liturgy with you into your everyday world.

Strategies for Different Age Groups

Refer to the section in your text on God's creation.

- With primary-age learners you can use a children's Bible to talk about the gifts of creation and how we are to care for them. You might bring in (or ask them to bring in) pictures of persons or events for whom you can pray. Ask your learners what they can do to help others. Use songs and activities that help relate creation and the liturgy to their lives. Include some moments of silence during your session, however brief, to help them learn to reflect and listen to God's voice. Guided meditations, according to age level, also offer an opportunity to help them "listen."

- Share with your intermediate-age children some facts about poverty in our country and in the world (visit www.intothefields.org for links), as well as activities that emphasize the message. Pray and decide together what you might do to help. Use faith sharing on the Sunday Scripture to help the children hear what God is asking them to do during the week. Have them make a banner celebrating God in creation.

- With your middle school children point out the moments of silence during the liturgy and explain their purpose (for example, during the penitential rite, after the readings and homily, after communion). Invite them to do an interview on the topic: How do you listen to God's voice in your everyday life?

- For youth, high school students, adults, and intergenerational gatherings, you could set up Learning Centers on the theme of listening to God, using the reflections in the above section for ideas. Ask them to work in groups to prepare prayer services on specific themes related to the topic of listening to God, then use the prayer services at your sessions. Invite them to discern the needs there are in your area and what God might be calling them to do as part of the parish's outreach ministry or some other form of outreach.

As You End This Session

During the week be attentive to the action of God in your life and in the lives of your learners.

Integrating What You Have Just Learned

- ***Share with other catechists the results of your formation session on finding God in creation. Reflect on your own experiences. What worked? What wasn't successful and why? Write down your thoughts.***

Notes

tips

- Provide moments of silence during your religion sessions: during prayer time, after reading Scripture, after or during an activity, and so on.

ON YOUR OWN

- *How can you best make use of the times of silence provided in the liturgy?*

God with Us

Do Not Be Afraid

In this exercise we will again use a kind of prayer that St. Ignatius calls "contemplation." Using the power of our imagination, we enter a Scripture passage, not only to understand it, but beyond that, to actually experience it in our own hearts. This kind of prayer takes the story beyond its surface details and lets it come alive for us. We become participants.

First, find a quiet place and put yourself in the presence of God. You're already familiar with this way of beginning an exercise.

Then ask God for the grace you desire. In this exercise it is the grace to know Jesus in a deeper way and understand the wonder and mystery of a God who takes flesh in our world.

Next, read the Scripture text slowly through once.

In those days a decree went out from Emperor Augustus that all the world should be registered.... Joseph also went from the town of Nazareth in Galilee to Judea, to the city of David called Bethlehem, because he was descended from the house and family of David. He went to be registered with Mary, to whom he was engaged and who was expecting a child. And she gave birth to her firstborn son and wrapped him in bands of cloth, and laid him in a manger, because there was no place for them in the inn.

In that region there were shepherds living in the fields, keeping watch over their flock by night. Then an angel of the Lord stood before them, and the glory of the Lord shown around them, and they were terrified. But the angel said to them, "Do not be afraid; for see—I am bringing you Good News of great joy for all the people: to you is born this day in the city of David a Savior, who is the Messiah, the Lord. This will be a sign for you: you will find a child wrapped in bands of cloth and lying in a manger." And suddenly there was with the angel a multitude of heavenly host, praising God and saying, "Glory to God in the highest heaven, and on earth peace among those he favors!"

So they went with haste and found Mary and Joseph, and the child lying in the manger. When they saw this, they made known what had been told them about this child; and all who heard it were amazed at what the shepherds told them. But Mary treasured all these words and pondered them in her heart. The shepherds returned, glorifying and praising God for all they had heard and seen, as it had been told them (Luke 2:1–20).

What meaning does the Incarnation hold for you?

■ *Now put the text down, close your eyes, and use your imagination to picture the scene with as much detail as you can. Look around to see what things look like. What does it smell like? Who is there? Picture the young Mary and Joseph. What are they doing? Look into their eyes. Place yourself in the scene, either as one of the characters or simply as a bystander. Begin to hear what's being said and watch the faces as the events unfold. Let the story proceed however your imagination takes you. The details of the text are not important. If something seems significant, savor it and don't hurry to move on. Most of all let your heart feel what's going on.*

■ *Don't get discouraged if nothing seems to be happening. Sometimes God lets us feel barren and empty to help us realize that it is not in our own power to experience consolation. Sometimes God is very close to us at these moments when we seem unable to pray. Try to spend 30-45 minutes with this part.*

When you have finished this exercise, write some of the images that helped you enter this Scripture passage in a prayerful way. What did you see, feel, smell, experience?

Notes

■ ***When it seems appropriate, listen to the song "Prince of Peace" (track 9 on the CD) and let it wash over you as you contemplate the birth of Jesus. Let yourself sit in silence for a few minutes at the end to rest there in the beauty and goodness of God.***

■ ***Here are the lyrics to the song:***

A mother holds a newborn babe
cradled in her arms.
She watches him with a mother's love,
her tiny, princely child.

A tiny hand reaches out to feel
the wonders of her face.
He plays a game with her smiling eyes,
her tiny, princely child.

Do not be afraid. I bring you news
of great joy.
For to you is born a Savior
who is Christ, who is Christ,
the Lord.

And who would think that this little child
could really be a king,
the Prince of Peace, the Promised One,
the Savior, Christ the Lord?

The blind shall see, and the deaf shall hear,
the lame shall leap for joy.
The hills will break into happy cries,
the heavens clap their hands.

■ ***Now take a few minutes to write about your listening experience. Did this help your contemplation experience? In what ways?***

Song Notes

Where do you find the face of Christ?

■ ***Now slowly and prayerfully read the following reflection.***

Human Meets the Divine

Sometimes the hardest part of the story of Jesus' birth is its familiarity. The act of God taking human flesh is an act of intimacy. It is a story of a God who is so in love with us that we can barely fathom it. We feel uncomfortable with this kind of closeness to God because we feel unworthy. Furthermore, to speak of God in such human terms can seem inappropriate, if not blasphemous. And yet this is what we Christians do. The infinite, all perfect God is presented to us as a human infant, born in a lowly cattle stall to poor parents of no great importance. Such is the foolishness of God's wisdom!

In the person of Jesus, spirit and matter are at once united. The divine permeates the universe of material things in such a way that the created world is set on a course of becoming more and more divine. As the divine God takes on our humanity, so our humanity begins to take on more and more of God's divinity. The work and power of God's redemption of this world is set in place.

During Advent, we don't go about pretending that Jesus the Christ has yet to be born. Rather, we're acknowledging our deep hunger and longing for God and the fulfillment of his promise. And Christmas is not just about re-telling the Christmas story and celebrating Jesus' birth. This is not just an event that took place only once in human history. To those who see with the eyes of faith, God continues to take flesh for us in thousands of unexpected ways and faces. This is what Ignatius of Loyola in his *Spiritual Exercises* calls "finding God in all things."

Why would the infinite God even want to bother with us? If God chose to reveal himself as an innocent, defenseless infant, there's no telling where we might find him taking flesh for us. We may experience the shepherds' disbelief when told that the long-awaited Messiah would be found wrapped in bands of cloth in a cattle manger. This may be one of those moments when silent adoration is our best response.

The Time of Prayer

Begin by listening once more to the song. At the end, spend a few minutes speaking to God using the prayer given here, or, better yet, use your own words.

The grace of contemplation is deepened when we take the images and persons of our prayer with us into our daily lives. So, as you go through your week, remember what you experienced in your time of prayer. Let the words and images be with you as you work, play, study, eat, and pray. Listen to the song during the week. Take it with you in the car, play it as you work around the house or before you go to bed. This will bring you back to the grace of this contemplation.

Great and infinite God,
your desire to be close to humanity overwhelms me.
Why would you even want to bother with us?
I kneel beside the manger crib to see this tiny infant,
the beauty of God in the flesh, so simple, so divine.
My heart sometimes doesn't know how to take it all in,
and with Mary I try to hold it all in the quiet of my heart.
Dear Lord, give me the eyes of faith
so that I might recognize you
whenever and wherever you take flesh for me.

When you are ready, end by praying the Our Father.

The Growing Faith Project booklets for this session are #10 and #30.

10 Sin and grace

Content summary of booklet #10

- *We were created to live in paradise and be near God.*
- *From the beginning we have experienced an inclination to be selfish and unilateral. This is called "original sin."*
- *As a result of original sin, human nature is weakened and inclined to sin.*
- *Everyone experiences original sin.*

This booklet makes reference to articles 374–421 in the *Catechism of the Catholic Church*.

30 We are destined for God

Content summary of booklet #30

- *As human persons we are from the moment of our conception destined to be with God and to enjoy eternal happiness.*
- *We are obliged to follow the moral law, which urges us "to do what is good and avoid what is evil." This law makes itself heard in our conscience.*
- *The Beatitudes help us respond to the desire for happiness that God has placed in our hearts.*
- *Our right to the exercise of freedom stems from our human dignity. This does not, however, give us the right to say or do anything we please.*

This booklet makes reference to articles 1691–1748 in the *Catechism of the Catholic Church*.

Excerpt from booklet #10

The reality of evil

One need not look any further than the daily newspaper
to see that evil exists in our world.
Who can escape it?
And yet...
Divine Love is infinitely good and holy.
All of Creation is good.
So, where does evil come from?
To fully understand sin,
we must examine our relationship to God.
For it is this relationship,
based in love and harmony,
that we reject in favor of our own futile desire.

On its bottom line,
sin is an abuse of the freedom to love
which God imparts to us all.

By sin we lost our original holiness.

Moving from Experience to Faith

Goal, Objectives, and Skill

The goal of *Moving from Experience to Faith* is to explore how we can best engage the life experiences of our learners to help them grow in faith, in conversion, and in commitment to Christ.

Your objectives are

- to help learners move from life experiences to better knowledge of themselves and of God (following Jesus' example in using experience in his teaching); in turn, faith will shed light on their experiences;
- to teach learners that sinful experiences can lead them away from God;
- to learn methods for incorporating the life experiences of learners in your sessions.

Skill

- Help learners move from experience to faith, and show how faith helps them interpret experience.

Preparation

- **Step One:** Experience the material in the *Spiritual Exercises*, and write your reflections.
- **Step Two:** Read booklets #10 *Why Do People Turn Away from God?* and #30 *What Makes Us Free?* of the *Growing Faith Project*. Do the reflections and exercises, recording your reflections.
- **Step Three:** Read *Tools for Teaching* carefully. Either at the group meeting or on your own, record your reflections and applications. If you are studying with a group, share your experiences in teaching sessions.

Connecting Sessions

After studying in the last session how to help your learners listen to God's voice, you will now focus on helping them use their life experiences to grow in faith.

Step One: Setting the Tone

This exercise gives you an example of how you can use a life experience in your religion sessions. Ask your learners to imagine the following scene.

You are having a special Sunday meal together because a relative has come for a visit. What kinds of food might your family prepare? Will you decorate the table and the room? Do you invite other relatives to your meal? With what other customs does your family celebrate special occasions?

How is celebrating the Eucharist like a special family meal? What makes it different?

> Catechesis helps people relate the Christian message to the most profound questions in life.
>
> NDC 29A

Step Two: Importance of This Session

This section introduces the importance of connecting life experience with catechesis. Read this on your own. If you take part in the group sessions, share your reflections with your group.

How can you help learners link their daily experiences with their faith life?

- Lead learners from their experiences to a better knowledge of themselves and of God, following Jesus' example in using experience in his teaching. Also show them how faith sheds light on their experiences.
- Illustrate for the learners how poor choices can lead to negative experiences which can lead us away from God.
- Learn methods for incorporating the life experiences of learners in your sessions.

Children often surprise us with the insights they glean from experience, insights that can be profound and at the same time humorous. For example, once a catechist was reviewing with her children the lesson they had studied the week before about God being all-powerful. The catechist asked, "Is there anything God can't do?"

There was silence. Finally one boy held up his hand. The catechist was disappointed because she thought the point of the lesson had been missed.

"All right, Kevin," she said resignedly, "just what is it that God can't do?"

"Well," the boy replied, "God can't please everybody."

As catechists and teachers we recognize the need to relate our own personal experiences to our faith and to our relationship with God. So, too, we foster the same awareness in our learners. It is important that we encourage learners to connect faith with life and life with faith. We don't learn about God in a vacuum. Rather, in our search for ultimate meaning in our lives, in seeking to understand better who God is for us, we bring the wisdom of our faith to shed its light on our searching. This searching is filled with the joys and sorrows, pleasure, and traumas of our lives. It is filled with positive and negative experiences, the good and the poor choices of our daily lives. It is in making our way through life that we raise questions about the meaning of our existence, about good and evil in the world, and so on. Jesus knew how important experience was in teaching about the kingdom, about God, about the life he came to share with us, the life which is the Father's will for all people. When we reflect on the teachings and parables of Jesus, we find constant references to the life experience of the people of his time.

Integrating What You Have Just Learned

- ***If you were going to teach about God as being all-powerful, what experiences in the lives of your learners would you begin with? What activities or methods could you use, keeping in mind the age of your learners? Write your reflections below.***

Notes

tips

- The effectiveness of our ministry often depends a great deal on the ways in which we first discovered God.
- Experience can lead us into deeper dimensions of the mysteries of faith.

ON YOUR OWN

- *How often do you reflect on your own experiences to discern where God is acting in your life?*

Step Three: Experience and Faith

Jesus used the experiences of his listeners to teach them about the kingdom. Read this on your own. If you take part in the group sessions, share your reflections with your group.

Remember the movie *Pay it Forward?* Haley Joel Osmet plays the role of a young boy being raised by a single mom. He is influenced by his teacher (played by Kevin Spacey) to come up with a project that would make a difference in the lives of people. The project involves anticipating people's good and choosing to reach out and help them before they do anything to deserve such help. The film reminds us of many gospel stories about seeds—the gospel of faith the size of a mustard seed, the gospel of seeds planted and growing without our awareness or attention.

Encourage the learners to move from experience to faith. Have them consider their own life experiences in relation to the gospels. Jesus used very down-to-earth images: water, salt, fig trees, a vineyard, a dissolute son, a shepherd. With these examples and others, he helped people find God in their own experiences, to see God in the smallest events and elements of their lives. And he used these experiences to prepare their minds and hearts for belief in him and in his message of conversion, love, and salvation.

ON YOUR OWN

- *In what images or experiences of your life have you touched the mystery of God?*

Jesus taught about hope and love in the parable of the Good Samaritan (Luke 10:29–37). He taught about the meaning of life in the Sermon on the Mount (Matthew 5–7) and in the description of the final judgment, when he rewards those who fed the hungry and gave drink to the thirsty (Matthew 25:31–46).

Invite the learners to memorize facts about the faith, to learn the Creed, and to know their prayer formulas. Remind them that if they do not make what they learn about the faith come alive in their own daily lives, these facts will not help them become disciples of Jesus.

When we see a rainbow or any beautiful thing, we're apt to cry out, "There's God!" We feel God at those moments and can say it. Help your learners find God in the "rainbows."

Integrating What You Have Just Learned

- ***Choose a parable and discuss in a group or reflect on your own: What images does Jesus use in the parable? What is he teaching?***

Notes

Step Four:
Turning Away from God

Because we are free to choose, we can experience sin also. Read this on your own. If you take part in the group sessions, share your reflections with your group.

A part of our human experience is to sense the temptation to "the dark side," sin. Discuss with your learners how deep disappointments, loss, serious injury, even more than the weaknesses in our nature, can be occasions for us to turn away from God, from our relationship with God. And because we are free beings, we can make that choice. We can choose to live without God, to live without love for others, while we seek our own satisfaction.

Our participation in the liturgy of the Church, especially the sacraments of baptism, Eucharist, and reconciliation, help us recognize our weakness and at the same time strengthen our resolve to choose the path to conversion, with the help of the prayers of the community and the grace of God. Still, we may struggle with the "shadow side" of our lives. Jesus spoke of this experience in parables also. In fact, in the well-known parable of the prodigal son, we read about the experience of a young man who chooses to leave his family to pursue a life of pleasure and selfishness. As is the experience of many people who feel that they have "hit bottom" and then look closely at their lives, it is only when the son runs out of money that he realizes his error and repents. He begins his journey back to a father who has already forgiven him.

> Jesus consistently used the ordinary human experiences of daily life to form his disciples.
>
> NDC 29A

Use examples from Scripture to illustrate for your learners the power of freedom and the effects of making wrong choices. You can also share how wrong experiences lead to errors in judgment and in choices. The young man in the parable, for instance, may have been influenced by the example of others.

Through stories from Scripture like the prodigal son parable, combined with reflections on their own experiences, you can help learners realize that even if they turn away from God, God does not turn away from them. God always loves them and offers the grace of conversion.

Integrating What You Have Just Learned

- ***Choose two parables such as the story of the prodigal son or the one of the farmer sowing seeds that illustrate how people make wrong choices. What motivated them? How might the parable have ended if their choices had been different? Write down your reflections.***

Notes

ON YOUR OWN

- *Recall occasions when you were tempted to follow your own interests rather than love of God and the good of others. How do you feel now about those experiences? Did they help you grow in any way? How?*

Step Five: Faith Is a Verb

This section offers several ideas for connecting experience with catechesis. Read this on your own. If you take part in the group sessions, share your reflections with your group.

Examining how Jesus used experience has already given you some ideas about how learners' experiences can be a catalyst for their growth in faith. You want your learners to know that God, that Jesus, that faith is real—in every pore of their body, through every sense they are blessed with. The following suggestions offer further opportunities.

- Begin from the *actual experience* of the learners. Set up a scenario, as we did in Step One, and ask questions. Bring in an object and ask if the object reminds them of any experiences they have had. Ask them to draw a picture of a certain type of experience and talk about it. Invite them to list qualities they admire in a person and why. Begin with the experience of a prayer ritual. Talk about their experience of a rite or ritual in the liturgy. Ask them to share special seasonal observances or traditions in their families. Let the learners talk about something that happened to them during the week, making sure they don't speak of matters that are confidential or too personal. Then connect these experiences to the topic you are going to teach. Or, in the case of the last method, help them find God's presence in those experiences, then relate their experience to the topic.

> The catechist must teach the person to read their own lived experiences so as… to discover more and more God's plan for them.
>
> GDC 152c

- Use *appropriate activities* that engage learners' imaginations and, mindful of the principles of multiple intelligences that we studied in Session 5, engage as many of their senses as possible. Read or let your learners read a story from Scripture, or a story from children's literature. Find out through discussion how they relate to it. Have them role play the story, retell it, or use puppets or figures to act it out. Invite them to illustrate the story or write a poem on the topic. Sing a song, possibly with gestures, related to it. Play a game. Engage them in a simple craft that helps them learn about the topic. Then move from these experiences into the topic of your session.

- Let learners *pray over a recent event*—happy or tragic—then invite them to reflect on the meaning of it. Their prayer can be about something that happened to one of them, or an event in the neighborhood, country, or world.

- According to their age level, invite learners to be involved in *acts of service*. They can then reflect on the experience and what it meant for them.

- Use *different forms of prayer* and help learners become accustomed to reflection. If they are old enough, they can prepare and lead the prayer themselves. Again, engage as many of the senses as possible.

- With older learners, pose *moral dilemmas* appropriate for their age level. Invite them to discuss it in small groups, role play the situation, or journal about it, asking themselves what the gospel says about such a choice. Encourage them to provide examples, being careful again that they preserve confidentiality.

Whatever methods you use, you are aiming for your learners to experience a kind of revelation, for them to have a warm, alive, and creative knowledge of God, of their faith, and of their commitment to Christ.

Strategies for Different Age Levels

Learners of every age enjoy experiencing new things. You can use this to lead them to reflect on faith topics. Refer also to their text and your manual.

- Engage primary-age children in storytelling with motion. For example, play "Follow the Leader" to a Bible story, perhaps the story of Noah's ark. Then draw out the faith message as it relates to their lives. Use activity centers with objects related to different themes or teachings of the faith. Pray together about a recent event that has affected them directly or a tragedy that has affected the lives of many people.

- Invite intermediate-age learners to talk about a new or enjoyable experience they had during the week. Help them relate it to an area of Catholic faith or practice. Read an age-appropriate story or show a short video or DVD, or a clip, and ask the children to put themselves in the place of the characters. What would they have done?

- Ask middle-school learners to share in groups what they think about a particular new computer game. Does it reflect or go against gospel values? Ask them to tell the stories about their own experiences related to a faith topic. Invite them to work in groups and think about a situation when their peer group might try to pressure them to do something they know is wrong (smoke, take drugs, steal, cheat on an exam). Have them role play the situation with alternative endings.

- Invite youth, high school students, adults, or members of an intergenerational gathering to discuss in groups their experience of a new film or music CD. What are the messages it conveys? Are these in accord with or counter to the gospel? Ask them to come up with a slogan or even a song that conveys the message of one of the gospel parables or teachings. Have them keep track or estimate how much time their family spends together. What are some things families can do together to celebrate their faith?

As You End This Session

During the week, reflect on and write about experiences that caused you to question or to grow or to seek God in your faith.

Integrating What You Have Just Learned

- ***What methods have you used to help learners connect their life experiences to their faith? Record your reflections and ideas.***

Notes

tips

- Good literature and good art have a power to grasp the deep inner reality of things.
- Give your learners opportunities to play, dream, and pray.

Companions in Christ

Drawn by a Dream

This tenth exercise is a bit different from the previous ones. In each of the earlier exercises, we asked God for a particular grace that we wanted. Yet, God bestowed on us the grace that we most needed. St. Ignatius, in crafting his Spiritual Exercises, understood how important it is for a person to draw spiritual nourishment from the particular grace that God has given. Ignatius calls this experience "repetition."

With great love, God has bestowed an abundance of grace on you through these past weeks. This exercise does not present new material for reflection, but rather invites you to go back over the reflections you have already done in order to savor the powerful moments of grace that have been given you. You're invited this week to recall the graces you've been given, to relish them and find even more goodness in them.

This exercise might be a challenge and feel uncomfortable for some. We've been so conditioned to keep moving ahead and get on with the next task. Our culture is always on the go, not wanting to waste time. In the life of the spirit, however, remaining with any grace or consolation that's been given us is never a waste of time. It's a way of nourishing that deep down hunger we prayed about in our very first exercise.

O God, you are my God, I seek you,
My soul thirsts for you;
My flesh faints for you,
as in a dry and weary land where
there is no water.
(Psalm 63)

Prepare yourself now by closing your eyes and breathing deeply and slowly for a few moments. Rest for a moment in the presence of the God who loves you.

The next step is to go back and look at what you have written in this book for each of the previous exercises. Pay special attention to the notes you made at the end of each exercise. This is where you tried to put into words the special grace of that exercise for you. In the presence of God read through what you wrote. Allow yourself time to be grateful for what you've experienced. Then, in the space provided, make a list of the graces that are most important.

Notes

Abide in
my love
John 15:9

When you've finished, review what you've written. These are the things that you should spend more time with. For now, pick one of them. Remember back to that moment in the previous exercise and recall what it felt like. What was so significant about it? Why did it mean so much to you? Embrace it and savor it. Don't feel compelled to rush and move forward. Even if you spend the remaining time with this one grace and never finish the rest of this exercise, allow yourself the opportunity to bathe in God's infinite love and mercy. There's no need to figure anything out or draw a conclusion. Just be with God in the moment. Spend anywhere from ten to thirty minutes here before moving on.

When you're ready, continue with the reflection.

As a deer longs
for flowing streams,
so my soul longs for you,
O God.

Nothing is more practical than finding God, that is, than falling in love in a quite absolute, final way.

What you are in love with, what seizes your imagination, will affect everything. It will decide what will get you out of bed in the morning, what you will do with your evenings, how you will spend your weekends, what you read, who you know, what breaks your heart, and what amazes you with joy and gratitude.

Fall in love, stay in love, and it will decide everything.[1]

(Pedro Arrupe, SJ)

Lured by God's Love

Growing in the life of the Spirit is really about falling in love. It's about a personal relationship with Jesus. It's also, of course, about doctrines, moral principles, and being able to quote Scripture, but the first step is the encounter with Christ. The fact is, the almighty and infinite God, the Creator of this vast universe, is in love with you and hopes that you will fall in love with him. At their core, these exercises are about spending time with God, allowing ourselves time to get to know him, to see him in our daily lives and to hear him speak to us in our hearts and minds.

Have you ever seen a teenager in love? Their whole day revolves around the other person. That's all that's on their mind. They lose track of time and spend hours on the phone just talking about nothing. All they desire is to be in each other's presence. As we get a little older, we realize that falling in love might mean that we'll have to change our way of life, reveal ourselves to the other person in ways that we're not accustomed, allowing the other person to experience our selfishness and sinfulness. As we lose our innocence, falling in love can sometimes take more time.

This process of falling in love is what God has been doing within you through these exercises. Through grace God has been revealed to you and opened your heart to fuller love. God has been stretching your heart so that you can receive more love, and little by little, opening up the possibility that you will fall in love with him, too.

There are very few people who realize what God would make of them if they abandoned themselves into his hands, and let themselves be formed by his grace. (St Ignatius of Loyola)

[1] This quotation is attributed to Pedro Arrupe, S.J., Superior General of the Society of Jesus, 1961-1984.

Pilgrim Companions

We are not alone on our journey to let God's love transform us. We have many other travelers to stand with, men and women who have the same dreams, experience the same struggles, and hold on to the same hopeful promise. When we are discouraged, the faith of those other travelers can raise us up and give us the strength and desire to continue. God provides such pilgrims as a gift to us. They are men and women who desire, as we do, to know God more intimately, and so to fall in love with him.

■ ***Listen to the song "Pilgrim Companions" (track 10 on the CD) now. Its lyrics echo many of the themes and graces God has bestowed on you in these exercises.***

■ ***Here are the lyrics of the song:***

Drawn by a dream, lured by a love,
Pilgrim companions,
as friends on the journey
We come through the storm,
pass through the fire,
Hungry yet hopeful,
sustained by the love of the Lord.

Harken, O people, remember the journey
that brought us through flood
and through fire.
For the God who is gracious
has seen how we hunger
and fed us with bread for our hearts.

Over and over we hunger for someone
to feed us and fill our desire.
When the God of our longing
has courted and captured our hearts
we will hunger no more.

Daring to dance in the shadow of death;
willing to gamble a love for all time.

"Pilgrim Companions" by Dan Schutte. From the collection ***Drawn by a Dream***.

■ ***Now take a few minutes to write about your listening experience. Did this help your contemplation experience? In what ways?***

Song Notes

The Time of Prayer

■ ***Close your eyes and imagine God's face before you. God is proud and takes great delight in you. End with the following prayer, or better, with a prayer in your own words.***

■ ***The final part of this exercise is something that you'll take with you during the coming week. Go back and look at the list of graces and memories you made at the beginning of this exercise. Find a place in your home to put that list so that you will remember it. When you wake up, go to bed, drive, or make dinner, let these graces follow you. Take a moment to write down some concrete ways that will help you do this.***

Dear God, Lord of Love,
I sit here feeling nervous before the gaze of your love.
I'm not accustomed to letting you look at me in this way.
The power and depth of your love takes my breath away.
Forgive me if I'm not yet able to give myself to you completely,
not yet able to fall in love with you.
I can't even fathom what that would feel like.
Make up for what is lacking in my desire, Lord.
Let the fire of your love transform me
so that I can become a better disciple,
a better teacher and bearer of your Word.

When you are ready, end by praying the Our Father.

The Growing Faith Project booklet for this session is #48.

48 Praying as Jesus taught

Content summary of booklet #48

- *The Lord's Prayer is truly the summary of the whole gospel.*
- *The Lord's Prayer is the basic prayer of the Christian life.*
- *Praying to our Father should help us want to become like God and foster in us a humble and trusting heart.*
- *In the Our Father, the object of the first three petitions is the glory of the Father: the sanctification of his name, the coming of the kingdom, and the fulfillment of his will. The four others present our wants to God. They ask that our lives be nourished, healed of sin, and made victorious in the struggle of good over evil.*

This booklet makes reference to articles 2759–2865 in the *Catechism of the Catholic Church.*

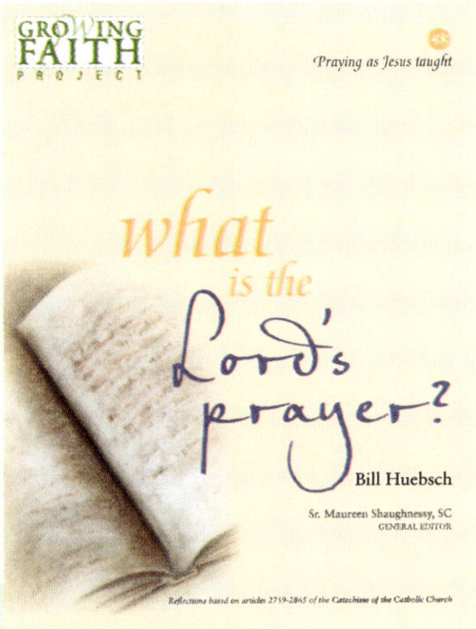

Excerpt from booklet #48

The gospel

In the gospels, Jesus' disciples knew him
to be a man of prayer.
Seeing how this touched and affected his life,
they asked him to teach them to pray as well
and in response, Jesus taught them
the fundamental Christian prayer.

We are sons and daughters of God
and we realize this is a privileged calling.
Thus the Lord's Prayer reveals us to ourselves
at the same time that it reveals the Father to us.
We are adopted by one who loves us eternally
and this creates within us two basic outlooks.

First, we desire to become like God,
full of love ourselves,
full of compassion and forgiveness.
Second, we learn to trust like a child does,
trust that God will give his children
what they ask in Christ's name.

The Lord's Prayer is a summary of the whole Gospel.

Summing Up

Goal

The goal of *Summing Up* is to review and integrate everything you have studied in the first nine sessions of *Into the Fields.*

Preparation

- **Step One:** Engage the material in the *Spiritual Exercises*, and write your reflections.
- **Step Two:** Read booklet #48 *What Is the Lord's Prayer?* of the *Growing Faith Project*. Do the reflections and exercises, recording your reflections.
- **Step Three:** Review the other nine chapters and complete the exercises in the Review section.

Step One: How to Sum Up

The aim of this session is to help you review and integrate all the material of the preceding nine sessions.

To help you review each session

- Make sure you study the Goal, Objectives, and Skills first.
- Read the notes you made for each section of, "Integrating What You Have Just Learned." These will help you call to mind the purpose of each session and what you took away from it.
- As you review the actual content of the session, give more attention to the body of the content than to the strategies. If you have not already done so, highlight important words, key phrases, or ideas.

Step Two: Review the Goal, Objectives, and Skills of the First Nine Sessions

Let them guide you in your review, as they are the main ideas, skills, and attitudes you took with you from the sessions. Read on your own or study with others.

Session One: The Call to Be a Catechist or Teacher

The goal was to help you deepen your understanding of your calling, which means knowing and following Christ and leading others to him.

Intended Objectives:

- to better understand the nature of catechesis;
- to emphasize and teach that discipleship is the outcome you seek in catechesis;
- to take the catechumenate as a model for fuller initiation into the life of Christ and the Church.

The skill was to sacrifice yourself as a catechist or teacher, working selflessly for your learners.

Session Two: Preparing a Learning Space

The goal was to help you make the learning space a sacred and welcoming environment for your learners.

Intended Objectives:

- to learn ways to prepare yourself carefully and prayerfully before each session;
- to learn how to promote an atmosphere in which all the learners feel welcome;
- to learn how to organize the learning space.

The skill was to prepare a welcoming, organized learning space for the learners.

Session Three: Planning the Learning Session

The goal was to help you see the importance of planning and preparing for the lesson ahead of time.

Intended Objectives:

- to learn how to set your goal and objectives;
- to learn how to plan effective lessons;
- to acquire different strategies for review and application.

The skill was to plan lessons effectively.

Session Four: Liturgy as a Teaching Moment

The goal was to help connect liturgy with catechesis.

Intended Objectives:

- to learn how to break open the word of God together with the learners;
- to learn how to bring the liturgy into the religion session effectively;
- to learn how to use mystagogy to teach about the experience of liturgy.

The skill was to live the liturgy so it would also be an important element of your teaching.

Session Five: Applying Principles of Development

The goal was for you to learn about the nature of learning, and the principles of developmental theory and multiple intelligences as applied to effective religious education.

Intended Objectives:

- to learn how to apply the principles of learning to faith formation;
- to acquire various methods to reach each learner;
- to learn how to apply the multiple intelligences approach.

The skill was to recognize the ongoing development of each learner and use methods suited to each one.

Session Six: Engaging Scripture Effectively

The goal was to help you make Scripture an integral part of your life and the lives of the learners.

Intended Objectives:

- to teach learners how to use the Bible, according to their age level, by presenting it as a library;
- to learn methods for teaching about sacred Scripture and using it in religion sessions;
- to help learners love Scripture and apply it to their lives.

The skill was to teach the learners to make Scripture part of their lives, especially by living their teachings in your own life.

Session Seven: Building a Community of Love

The goal was for you to determine how to build a community of love among your learners through respect, order, affirmation, and love for one another.

Intended Objectives:

- to formulate the rules of good conduct for the religion sessions, with the help of the learners, if possible;
- to learn about the different factors that might motivate a child to misbehave, and to treat behavioral issues as Jesus would;
- to learn ways to foster understanding, respect, communication, and collaboration among the learners.

The skill was to build a community of love among your learners, modeled after the communion of love of the Trinity and the example of Jesus.

Session Eight: Teaching Others as God Teaches Us

The goal was to make God's way of revelation a model for catechesis.

Intended Objectives:

- to understand the characteristics of God's self-revelation as a source and model for catechesis;
- to relate these characteristics to catechesis;
- to learn strategies to help learners recognize God's voice in their lives.

The skill was to listen to and learn from God's self-revelation in order to model our teaching on it.

Session Nine: Moving from Experience to Faith

The goal was for you to use the life experiences of the learners to help them grow in faith, in conversion, and in commitment to Christ.

Intended Objectives:

- to lead learners from their experiences to better knowledge of themselves and of God, following Jesus' example in using experience in his teaching; in turn to show how faith will shed light on their experiences;
- to teach learners that sinful behavior can lead them away from God;
- to learn methods for incorporating the life experiences of learners in your sessions.

The skill was to help learners move from experience to faith, and to let faith help them interpret their experiences.

Step Three: Exercises

The exercises in this section are not a test, although they will form part of your evaluation. They are a practical way of assisting you in absorbing and assimilating the material covered in this past year. In each section you will have two options. Choose one of the options and complete it as best you can.

Section I: Human Learning and Catechesis

Based on sessions one, five, and eight. Choose A or B.

Option A

1. Share what motivated you to become a teacher or catechist. What does catechesis mean to you? What does your ministry mean to you?

2. What stage of human and faith development, in general, have most of your learners reached? Briefly explain some characteristics of the way they learn. Choose one of your learners and illustrate his or her way of learning (one of the multiple intelligences). Do not use any names, however.

3. Explain two teaching methods you use with your learners and how they are modeled after the way God or Jesus teaches us.

Option B

1. How would you describe the ministry of catechesis to someone interested in becoming a teacher or catechist? Be convincing.

2. Discuss the stages of faith development and how they relate to catechesis. Briefly explain two of the multiple intelligences and provide an activity related to each one.

3. Describe at least three of the teaching methods Jesus used and give examples from the gospels.

Section II: Nuts and Bolts

Based on sessions two, three, and seven. Choose A or B.

Option A

1. Draw a simple plan of how you would envision your physical environment, including seating arrangement, placement of visuals, and so on.

2. Write up a detailed outline for a lesson plan on any topic you choose, following the format outlined in Session 3. Include your goal and objectives. Be sure to begin from the moment the learners enter the room until the moment they leave. Give your reasons for the activities you choose. Be sure to include prayer time.

3. What are the four qualities you need to foster and build a community of love? Include one behavior issue that might arise and how you would address it.

Option B

1. Provide the outline of an actual lesson you taught. Begin with the arrangement of your meeting space. Include your goal and objectives. Give a detailed account of how you presented the lesson, what activities you did, and so on.

2. Describe two things you do to build a community of love among your learners. Depict one behavior issue that arose, even if small. How did you resolve it?

3. What was your evaluation of the lesson? What did you learn from it?

Section III:
Using Experience, Scripture, and Liturgy in Catechesis

Based on sessions four, six, and nine. Choose A or B.

Option A

1. Describe in your own words the importance of connecting experience and catechesis. Give three examples of how Jesus used experience to teach his listeners, as portrayed in the gospels.

2. What are two ways you can use to teach your learners reverence for Scripture? Explain one specific activity you can use for each age level to teach the learners about Scripture.

3. Explain "mystagogy" and how its place in the catechumenal model of formation is instructive for how we engage in the ministry of catechesis. Provide two specific examples.

Option B

1. Discuss briefly the fact that a part of our human experience is to sense the temptation to the "dark side." How is this related to freedom and choice? Give two examples from Scripture. Then describe two specific activities (for any age) that help learners link life experience with faith.

2. What do we mean when we say that the Bible is a library? Describe how you get your learners excited about Scripture.

3. Discuss the importance of linking liturgy and catechesis. Describe two specific activities for teaching learners about the liturgical year.

Step Four:
Your Own Evaluation

After you complete the above exercises, note the areas you feel you need to return to for further study, explanation, or practice. After the session, discuss these areas with another catechist or teacher, or with your director or principal.

You can use these questions as a guideline.

- Did I need a lot of time to answer a particular question or questions? Why?
- Did I feel unsure about an answer or answers? Why?
- Was it hard for me to apply the points of the lesson to a teaching situation? Why?
- Which areas do I think I need to concentrate on most and why?